Creative Cooking

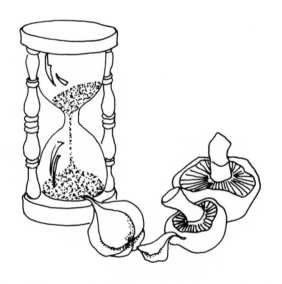

in 30 Minutes

OVER 380 IMAGINATIVE AND
DELICIOUS RECIPES FOR THE BUSY
COOK WHO LIKES GOOD FOOD

Sylvia Schur

SIMON AND SCHUSTER / NEW YORK

1   2   3   4   5   6   7   8   9   10

Library of Congress Cataloging in Publication Data

Schur, Sylvia.
    Creative cooking in 30 minutes.

    Includes index.
    1. Cookery. I. Title.
TX652.S37   641.5'55   75-2034
ISBN 0-671-21989-8

To Saul
for whom the pudding is the proof,
and the proof the pudding

Contents

Introduction

A half hour is all it takes to cook your choice of wonderful meals—if you choose with care. In one half hour you can produce a truly delectable meal, as satisfying to the eye as to your hunger. Why settle for less?

Many great classic recipes are quick to make. You see the proof of this when you order a specialty menu that is prepared by the maitre d' at your table; or when a Chinese or Japanese meal is cooked to your order; or when you dally over a drink while an omelet or a soufflé is prepared. Any of these is ready within thirty minutes.

The best and freshest foods are quickly prepared. Vegetables and fruits retain their vitamins and minerals; meats do not toughen to the point where they have to be retenderized by long cooking. Fish and seafood are tender and flavorful. Pasta is delicate, yet resistant to the bite.

Many of our lengthy cooking methods—stewing, braising and simmering—were designed to make older and tougher or dried foods more appealing, or to gelatinize tissues, or to cook very large chunks of meat. Some of these you may want to do on an occasional full day of cooking. I consider a stock pot an investment in good eating all week. But if you'd rather take to the hills instead of the kitchen on weekends, prepared broth can fill the bill for you. And if you use a pressure cooker or even a microwave oven, new time-expansion is open for your cooking—but you won't need either of these in the recipes that follow.

In the new life styles, elaborate meals and parties seem out of place. Simplicity is the essence of the new approach. While a morning or a day at the range may be creative and productive, the full-time kitchen slave has lost or left the role—often for a paycheck job outside the home.

The quality of the food you prepare finds its reflection in your own life. You (and your family) may lose more in gratification than in weight if you don't cook. You can be served at a restaurant, or pick up a take-out order—even dial for one, at a price. Or you can heat a frozen casserole and eat it from its container. And eat and eat, in search of missing flavor satisfaction . . . or identity.

Working live-aloners confess to frequent nonmeals—maybe nutritious, but hardly gratifying, "dinners" of peanut butter and bread, gulped while reading or sorting clothes for the laundromat. Some subsist on fat-trapped and nourishment-stripped nibbles.

In families, the separately eaten meal, or the TV-viewing meal, or the snack meal reduces the group to alone-ness. While the foods so used may be *part* of a sound eating scene, if they become the total they threaten self-identity as well as nutritional status. Calorie-laden nonmeals make for obesity. This kind of eating hardens the arteries of the spirit, too!

You can paint a better mealtime scene for yourself. Use awareness, a perceptive eye and practical shopping skills to bring a sense of the seasons and of beauty to your meals.

Walk home from work to spot a dinner "extra" or reach into your kitchen supplies to come up with a meal that reflects the day's discoveries. Choose a ginger-flavored omelet with green onions and crabmeat on Good Friday, a bowl of berries in summer or perfect apples in the fall; a steaming soup pot on a frosty day, seasonings cut from your windowsill herb pot, a dish you

design to match a mood. This is cooking as a salute to life—
your life.

It takes more will than skill to prepare a good, even a gourmet-
worthy, meal in half an hour—or in ten minutes—for one, or
two, or more. Make it sukiyaki or one-pot quick stew with salad
and beverage, or go the whole way with soup, main dish, vegetables, a made dessert, or fruit. Yes, and sit down to dinner
within the half hour—the abracadabra cook.

Serve your half-hour meal in an attractive setting, whether
you arrange it on a table or on a tray or on a bright cloth spread
over a box. If others share the food, let them share in the preparation and in the sensory perception of the flavors, colors, tex-
tures, aromas you achieve. Of all consciousness-expanding
experiences, the most universal comes with the relaxed inter-
change a satisfying dinner brings—all the more gratifying when
you pull it off within a half hour.

The first requisite for this satisfaction is that you *want* to prepare the meal (wanting to is a gesture of respect for yourself
and the others who will share it). Second, you need foods on
hand. Third, you need to know what to do with them. Read on.

We worked our way off the farm by devising intricate methods
of production and specialization—but most of us give little
thought to applying efficiency skills to our own life needs.

This book begins with money-saving shopping tips and practical techniques for quick meal planning in mind, goes on to
dovetailing preparations, and then into a complete cookbook of
recipes for every course, none of which takes more than a half
hour to prepare, and all of which can fit into complete thirty-
minute meals. Each recipe carries the times for preparation and
cooking. For practical preparation, couple one 15- to 25-minute
dish with one that takes only five minutes. Finally, there are
memorable dinner menus, including four buffets (one for each
season). Seven pattern menus for weight-watching are included;

but the basic scheme of this book is designed for sensible contemporary eating.

Here are 388 ways to great meals—each prepared within a half hour. They offer rewards that satisfy more than physical appetites. Enjoy!

1 How to Shop in Quick Time,
Save 20 Percent—and Eat Better Too

Food shopping is one household chore that pays off in immediate savings. You save by the very fact that you shop for food rather than eating out. Home-prepared food costs less than one-third its equivalent in a restaurant, and can offer better eating, too. You can feast on mushrooms, chicken breast supreme and berries for less than the price of a hamburger and a milk shake at a stand-up eatery.

And when you shop with care, you'll find still greater benefits. The nutritional quality of what you eat has little to do with what you pay. Flank steak makes a succulent meal in nine minutes, at about 30 percent less in cost than porterhouse. Lamb kidneys cook in one-third the time it takes to heat a frozen prepared macaroni casserole, at about half the price, with double the nutritional value. Discover the pleasures of vegetables bought in season (and at their lowest price), quickly braised or steamed to preserve their crispness. Use these for some of the meatless dishes included here. Pocket your savings and profit from the vitamin bonus.

You bite off something worth chewing when you shop with an eye to nutrition. Some of the costliest expenditures in food markets are for fluff or crunch or sip items with no real food value. Shop for the foods that serve your nutritional needs first—main-dish meat, poultry, fish or eggs, beans, nuts, cheese, dairy foods, fruits and vegetables, good grains. Then buy oil, vinegar, salt, seasonings, canned staples—the ingredients for efficient preparation. The combined savings on individual items you choose can add up to total savings of 20 percent or more on every dollar you spend, both for basic foods and convenience products, if you follow key rules for shopping.

The Meat of the Matter

The largest chunk of most food budgets goes for meat, so it pays to learn to save here. Usually the quick cook leans heavily on smaller tender cuts—steaks and chops, which are the most expensive cuts of meat. If you want to save, buy a beef roast, standing rib or sirloin, and have it sliced into steaks, freezing some for later use. The same applies to buying lamb. Chops off the top of a leg of lamb may cost fifty cents per pound less than chops bought by the piece. Or select a half-leg of lamb (the sirloin end) and have the whole cut into one-inch slices for delectable lamb steaks, to cook indoors or out. If you plan to cook a roast over the weekend, have a portion cut off in thin slices for other quick meals during the week.

There is no difference in the nutritional value of expensive and less expensive meats—except that the more expensive grades are interlarded with more fat. The difference has to do with tenderness and with demand. The most tender roasts, steaks and chops make up just 25 percent of the animal, and because of this they are expensive. But many less expensive cuts *can* be cooked tender in short order.

For example, not long ago cooks thought that flank steak had to be braised for at least an hour and a half—preferably longer. Frequently the steak was stuffed and rolled, then potted. This method of cooking toughens the muscle fibers and it takes two hours or more to soften them again. Yet you can broil the same flank steak as London Broil in just nine minutes and make one of the tastiest and most convenient dishes ever.

The secret in cooking less tender cuts of meat is to cook them quickly, until they are just rare. If they are cooked longer than that, they toughen, and long cooking will be required to tenderize them again. If you don't allow meat to toughen, you can enjoy tender, rare meats at a modest price.

Veal cut in thin slices from the leg, as for scaloppine, is a joy to the quick cook. It is no joy to the pocketbook, though! If you spot a shoulder roast of veal, or a rump on special, buy either one, and cut into thin slices or cubes for quick preparation.

Include pork, both fresh and smoked, in your timesaving meat choices. Fresh pork chops or shoulder, if cut into thin strips for Oriental or braised dishes, can be safely cooked in short order. Also, ham steak, bacon and sausage can be prepared quickly in interesting ways.

Remember lamb for good eating at practical prices. All parts of young lamb are tender and can be cooked quickly.

Specialty meats such as liver, kidneys and brains offer superior nutritional values and good economy in both cooking time and price.

Ground meat is obviously the quick cook's ace. Grinding does the pretenderizing, speeds cooking, allows for challenging variety in preparation and seasoning. For best value and flavor, choose flavorful ground chuck, rather than prepared hamburger mixtures, which are generally higher in fat content. But you might like to try ground lamb or a beef-and-veal combination for a change of pace.

Bird in Hand

Tender young broiler-fryer chickens, produced today at comparatively low cost per pound, can be fried, broiled, steamed, poached or even baked, within a half-hour's cooking time. The trick is to halve or quarter the chicken to allow for quick cook-through. For best buy in terms of cost per serving, buy whole chickens. A live-aloner can profit by dividing one bird into meal-sized freezer packs. Also, when you buy the whole bird you can build up a stockpile of chicken backs, giblets and necks for soup preparation. Freeze livers separately, too, for a quick and delectable meal.

If you choose to buy chicken parts, the breast is generally the most expensive per pound, but since it has the least waste, it is often the best buy. Boned chicken breasts can be used in a wide number of interesting recipes. Legs and thighs are next in price—and some think tops in flavor. Chicken wings are usually inexpensive, and can be grilled as a main dish or hors d'oeuvre. These are delicious when basted with barbecue or soy sauce. Necks and backs make an economical buy for soup or stew, although the actual cost of the meat itself is not as low as it would seem, because these are very bony pieces.

Turkey? Yes, especially if you buy parts such as economical turkey legs and thighs, which can be cut into smaller pieces for quick cooking. Or buy a boneless turkey roll, to slice for fast preparation.

Small Rock Cornish game hens are ideal choices for a quick company dinner. Buy these on sale, to store in the freezer and defrost as needed.

When time is really tight, precooked chicken, either from the store rotisserie or canned or frozen, comes to the rescue. This is one of the least expensive of precooked meats.

Fish Fast

The most time-consuming part of cooking up a fish feast may be finding your catch! Unless you are near the water, fresh fish has become increasingly scarce in recent years. Check frozen fish or canned fish or seafood for alternates. It takes no longer to cook fish than to heat some frozen precooked fish dishes—and you'll save money and gain in flavor if you prepare it yourself.

Harvest Your Values

While fresh fruits and vegetables offer some good buys at the peak of their season, you will actually spend less per serving on canned and frozen products most of the year.

Comparing prices, you are likely to find that frozen vegetables are less expensive than fresh, besides being precleaned for you; canned are often the least expensive. Yet you may want the fresh flavor, texture and nutritional values of the fresh, and may find these worth the difference in price. In supermarkets, prepackaged produce frequently is less expensive than that weighed to order. Smaller sizes usually offer savings over larger-sized fruits, and offer more pieces to the pound as well.

Shopping to Save

To make the most of your shopping time and dollars, follow these steps:

1. Set aside a regular hour for food shopping once a week, and buy in quantities to fill your weekly needs. This will avoid hurried and costly after-work shopping and expensive impulse buying.

2. Build up a "pantry" of staples and canned goods and check this before you go shopping. Decide on the number and menus of the week's meals and then buy basics accordingly. (For instance, if you're planning on a ham steak, you will want canned yams to go with it, and mustard for seasoning. And oh, yes, canned pea soup to extend the leftovers.)

3. Check your local store ads to see what specials are available before you shop. Take advantage of these when you do your menu planning.

4. Buy staples in economical form—in packages as large as you can conveniently store and use. To balance your expenditures, alternate large purchases in different departments each week.

5. Include some "backstop" foods in each shopping trip, such as canned tuna or other items to make an emergency meal. Include "backstop" staples as well, such as nonfat dry milk, for example, to guarantee a supply (and save about one-third in cost as compared with fresh milk).

6. Buy food in season—that's when it's plentiful and lowest in price. If possible, freeze some of your better buys for use later on.

7. Learn the layout of the store where you are going to shop, and plan your purchases accordingly. Begin with hard-packed staples from the grocery section, then buy baked goods, refrigerated items—meats, poultry, fish—fruits and vegetables, putting fragile items at the top of the cart. Pick up frozen products and ice cream just before checkout.

8. Some weeks, switch your shopping routine to stock up on specialties at other stores. These may be international foods, produce from a special market, delicatessen items from a pork store or unusual baked goods. You will enjoy the change in shopping procedure and your menus will reflect the different flavors.

9. Wherever you shop, read the labels, compare prices on different sizes of the same foods, to arrive at the best cost per serving. Check the unit prices for the cost per measure, to compare the actual costs of different brands and sizes.

10. Buy the quality that's appropriate for your use. You'll save if you choose tomato pieces for use in cooking, rather than the solid-pack tomatoes you may want for salads. The same applies to flake style vs. solid-pack tuna, and to

random size rather than uniform pack of peas.

11. Eggs are the making of many a quick meal—worth studying for economical buys. Eggs are priced by weight per dozen, and when there is a difference of seven cents or more per dozen between two sizes of eggs, the smaller size is the better buy. If there is a price difference between brown and white eggs, choose the less expensive—there is no difference in nutritional value between the two.

12. Keep in mind your varying time and meal-preparation needs in shopping for convenience foods as well as money-saving basics. For example, with baking potatoes, new potatoes to boil quickly, instant potatoes or potato pancake mix, and a package of frozen potatoes in sauce ready to heat and serve, you're ready to meet any mealtime situation with poise.

These twelve shopping rules have been tested again and again by shoppers in supermarkets in many parts of the U.S. By following these guidelines, shoppers have found that they can save up to 20 percent.

An hour spent in planned shopping once a week saves time, as well as money, as compared with scattered day-to-day shopping. This kind of shopping also enables you to work out more flavorful and more nutritious meals. In fact, having the food ready and waiting may *inspire* you to prepare meals you might otherwise skip, and entertain guests you might otherwise forego.

2 How to Plan a Meal and Organize Your Menu with Ease

Composing a meal in short order combines the rhythmic sense of a musician and the efficiency of a traffic manager. Both skills take practice—and readiness.

The meal organization which begins in the supermarket continues when you store food at home, and it is better executed in a well-organized kitchen.

Set up a food-assembling and preparation spot where the tools, equipment and seasonings you need most often are close at hand. Have a handy board or counter space for chopping, cutting, wrapping, with rubbish disposal nearby.

Store to Use

When you bring foods home from the supermarket, store them in as close to usable form as possible. If you have bought a large quantity of rice or beans, for example, put away the bulk, and set what you will need for more immediate meal preparation closer to the front of the cupboard or shelf. It is handy to keep small amounts of frequently used cooking ingredients, such as flour, sugar, salt, bread crumbs, cornstarch, oil and vinegar, favorite herbs and spices, in a storage unit close to where you prepare foods.

Always store staples in the same spot. You will save time if you always know exactly where these are. To save fumbling, arrange spices and herbs in alphabetical order, or group them according to type. Clean greens when you bring them home and wrap in moist paper or terry towels, to store in refrigerator hydrator. Fresh parsley and other herbs keep well, washed and placed in a screw-topped jar with just the moisture that clings to the leaves. To store meats and fish in the freezer, wrap in cooking-portion packets; preshape burgers and pack with separators between each; season and shape meat loaf before freezing. Freeze-and-cook wraps save time and motion in preparation.

Bread keeps fresher in the freezer than in the refrigerator. Divide breads and rolls into practical units for your use, wrap in clear plastic bags, then freeze to use as needed.

Even a small freezer can hold a cache of cooking assists: consommé or stock frozen in blocks, prepared pastry shells, fruits for pie filling or ready-to-bake pies, meats, fish and poultry, vegetables, sauces, sausage, fresh cranberries for a quick sauce, even fresh ginger, which grates perfectly from the frozen state.

Enjoy the makings of good meals as part of your decorative scheme. A pot of chives adds a green note to your windowsill, even while you clip it regularly for cooking. Delicate dill makes a fragrant bouquet for the kitchen table, and adds a lift to soup or salad or morning omelet, as well as to fish. A bowl of fruit is a centerpiece, then dessert. Complement the fruit with eggplant and squash, rosy peppers and ripening tomatoes, for beauty before cooking and satisfying, varied meals afterward.

Of Time and Motion

The most efficient kitchen planning takes the form of a triangle in which you move from refrigerator to sink to preparation center close by, to range. Set up another spot at a midway point for completed foods, and to line up dishes and tableware. You will save motions if you use a tray to collect these items and bring them to the table. Use the same tray to carry dishes back to the sink.

Make it a habit to plan at least the main portion of your dinner immediately after breakfast—even if you leave for work early. Five minutes spent in planning in the morning can save much more in time and frustration in the evening! As a bonus, you will find you move through the day with anticipation and choose your lunch far more satisfactorily.

For example, if you plan to cook peppers and pork, Chinese style, and the pork is hard-frozen, pop it into the refrigerator, to partially defrost for cutting into thin slices. You could serve this with quick-cooking bland rice made when you come home in the evening. But if you have a pot of water boiling for your morning coffee, it is easy to pour boiling water over brown (whole-grain) rice, add salt, return to boil, turn off, then let this stand all day. When you come home, the rice will have absorbed the water (page 140) and will need only heating for satisfying good eating. If you have the time, assemble other staples you will need for your meal.

Relax to Go

When you arrive home, take a few minutes to relax before you go into final preparations. Change into clothes you will enjoy for dinner and the evening. Put a kettle of water on to boil, fix a tray with an appetizer and drink, even something as simple as tomato juice. You will be ready to prepare your meal with more ease and efficiency—even serenity. So will the others who will share the dinner.

Playing the Timer

It pays to work with a kitchen timer, at least until you get the hang of timing your preparations. Having chosen your main course first, plan the remainder of the meal according to the time it takes for preparation and cooking. If you are preparing a main-course soup, for example, that takes five minutes to assemble and fifteen minutes to simmer before adding a final garnish, you have fifteen minutes in which to do a complex salad; or you might decide to bake some quick corn sticks, and settle for a bowl of lettuce and cucumber as salad.

Begin with the dish that will take the longest to prepare, then dovetail other preparations in the intervals of cooking that dish. If your main dish requires considerable preparation and little cooking time—sukiyaki, for example—plan on a dessert that takes little or no preparation—say, mandarin orange sections with a dash of Cointreau added at the table, or kumquats in their own syrup.

Composing a Meal

A good meal satisfies a complex set of needs—physical, emotional, esthetic, practical. You want to take all this into account within the half-hour preparation time available.

To simplify this, consider that all the dishes labeled "main course" in this book meet about one third of the day's protein needs for an adult. This is true of the hearty soups and salads and of vegetable main dishes, as well as the meats, fish and poultry.

Many of the main courses here are meals in one dish, to simplify preparation, serving, and clean-up too. These include protein and one or more vegetables. In other cases, your nutritional needs will be met if you add a side dish and a vegetable and/or salad. For children, include milk with each meal. Add bread or whole-grain crackers to your taste, and to satisfy caloric needs.

If your meal does not include salad, plan on fruit for dessert. You will find the dessert chapter heavy on fruits. Consider this a bonus of flavor, color and seasonal refreshment, as well as good nutrition.

Plan on contrasts of color, flavor and texture within the menu, and your nutritional needs are more likely to be filled, while you enjoy a more attractive meal within your half-hour preparation.

Tools and Time

It pays to invest in efficient cooking tools to help speed preparation, and for your own satisfaction in what you do. Sharp knives are a must: a chef's knife with a sturdy triangular base speeds chopping on a board; a covered chopping unit simplifies cutting onions, peppers and other small-quantity preparations. Include a serrated knife for cutting partially frozen vegetables. I also swear by a small curved boning knife for meats and a small band saw to help cut down larger units for quick cooking.

Add, in the cutting department, efficient kitchen shears to snip parsley and other herbs quickly; a sharp grater for nutmeg and ginger; a blender to speed many cutting and mixing chores dramatically. I like to keep all the cutting tools, grater and bottle-jar opener on a magnet over the cutting board; the blender stands on the rear of the same board, within handy reach of the sink, too.

Pans with a Purpose

It pays to select a variety of individual pans for special cooking purposes. Skillets are most important for the quick cook—and I include in this category a wok, the wide two-eared Chinese cooking pan with deep sloping sides. You should have a quick-heating skillet, possibly copper-bottomed, for quick browning; and a heavy skillet for even cooking. A well-seasoned omelet pan (rubbed with salt after using, not washed) is a joy to use. So is a fish poacher. Oven- or range-to-table pans save time in clean-up as well as preparation.

"From Scratch" in Short Order

Shortcuts? Yes, of course, instant onions and garlic salt save time. I just don't think they taste as good as fresh. Wherever preparation "from scratch" can be done within thirty minutes, that is the procedure included here. Where this cannot be done, as for example in cooking beans for mixed dishes, partially prepared products of good quality are suggested. If you want to save still more time by using the "instants," you will be that much more ahead.

On Coping

Our daughter Jane, who is a third-generation cook with little time to spare, and who has a keen editorial eye, suggested this addition.

When you don't have (or want to switch)	*Substitute*
1 *cup cake flour*	⅞ *cup all-purpose flour plus* 2 *tablespoons cornstarch* (*omit the cornstarch if you don't have it*)

1 tablespoon cornstarch or potato starch	2 tablespoons flour
1 cup butter	1 cup margarine or 7/8 cup hydrogenated fat or oil or drippings
1 cup honey	1¼ cups sugar plus ¼ cup water
1 cup brown sugar	7/8 cup granulated sugar plus 2 tablespoons molasses
1 ounce unsweetened chocolate	3 tablespoons cocoa plus 1 tablespoon fat
1 cup heavy cream	¾ cup milk plus ⅓ cup sweet butter
sour cream	yogurt, or sweet cream plus 3 tablespoons yogurt to the cup, or whirl cottage cheese with buttermilk to moisten in blender
1 cup buttermilk or sour milk	1 tablespoon vinegar or lemon juice plus sweet milk to make 1 cup (let stand 5 minutes)
1 cup nuts	1½ to 2 cups crisp cereal
thin cuts of meat	slice chicken breast or turkey, raw; or use bean curd or cheese slices
shrimp	thin strips of frozen fish fillets

1 teaspoon baking powder	¼ teaspoon baking soda plus ½ teaspoon vinegar or lemon juice used with milk to make ½ cup (let stand 5 minutes); or ¼ teaspoon baking soda plus ⅜ teaspoon cream of tartar
refined flour	whole-grain flour, in quantity reduced by ⅛, and reduce sweetening somewhat; molasses, less sweet than sugar, is very compatible

Shortcuts in Recipe Preparation

PEELING: *Potatoes, carrots, parsnips, beets:* Scrub with a brush and cook with skins on. If you want to peel, this is easier after cooking. Plunge into cold water and slip off skins. Even fried and broiled potato slices are good with the skins on, and more nutrients are preserved.

Mushrooms: Don't peel them. Wipe clean with damp cloth and cut off stem ends.

Apple Sauce: Simply quarter apples and cook with about 1 inch of water in pan, to prevent scorching. Put through food mill after cooking. Bonus: extra flavor and red skins color the applesauce pink, seeds and skins add flavor.

PRE-BROWNING: Turn vegetables and meats in hot fat briefly to glaze and seal in juices. Where flavor is appropriate, and darker color is desired in finished dish, add a little soy sauce or burned sugar or coffee, and heat to blend.

QUICK SAUCE THICKENER: Knead equal parts soft butter and flour with your fingers to combine, and add a tablespoon of mixture to cup of sauce, bring to boil, stirring until thickened.

To thicken with cornstarch, stir starch with a little cold water or wine or other liquid before adding to hot liquid. OR skim surface fat and serve au jus, or whirl in blender with vegetables used in cooking (onion, carrot, mushrooms) for rich flavor.

For cream sauce: Use cream—no thickening needed.

SIEVING OR PUREEING are not essential to most recipes; they add smooth texture, but don't change the basic flavor.

TO SPEED UP GELATIN-SET RECIPES, dissolve gelatin base in ¼ hot liquid, then add ice cubes, frozen concentrates or ice cream. Or, briefly place in the freezer to speed setting.

TO BOIL WATER FASTER, use a wide pan or kettle, cover, add salt where appropriate.

TO GRATE QUICKLY, whirl pieces in blender. Especially good for bread crumbs, grated cheese, herbs, onions, potatoes, chocolate.

About Utensils

Certain good tools are indispensable. It pays to invest in well-balanced knives with sharp blades; sturdy, heavy bowls; pans in various sizes and shapes; a broad-bottomed water kettle that hugs the heat; a good sieve, colander and steamer; a blender; a ceramic drip coffee pot; a pepper mill, grater, whisk and beater, kitchen scissors, rolling pin, cleaver.

If you don't have	*Use*
rolling pin	*straight-sided round bottle, such as a wine bottle*
cookie cutter	*glass or cup with thin edge*

sieve	cheesecloth or clean sink cloth stretched across pan; or hold lid against pan rim to allow water to flow out, retaining solids; or pour cool liquid through your fingers
sifter	toss dry ingredients to blend
double boiler	Rarely needed—just use very low heat. Or, set heatproof bowl, or a smaller pan, in larger pan ¼ filled with simmering water
garlic press	mash garlic together with salt, using flat side of knife blade
pastry blender	two knives, or your fingers
tart pans	form heavy-duty foil around pastry, set on rack to bake
beater	fork for eggs; your hand for cakes and batters—the best, quickest and "handiest" of all tools!

3 *Appetizers on Tap*

For the cook with little time, an appetizer is more than a tasty nibble to whet appetites for the meal to come. It serves as a speedy welcome to diners and allows the cook a little breathing space to get the main course under way. These appetizers say all's well. Any one of them makes a quick and satisfying prelude to the meal ahead. A variety would make a delicious spread for a party.

Make sure you keep ingredients on hand for these good, quick-to-fix appetizers. From A to Z—canned anchovies to fresh zucchini (thinly sliced these make great low-calorie dippers)—here is an array of appetizers you can set out with little or no preparation.

ANCHOVIES AND RED PEPPERS

Preparation Time: 2 minutes
Cooking Time: None

1 *jar (5 ounces) roasted red peppers (or fresh tomato slices)*

1 *can (2 ounces) anchovy fillets packed in oil*

On each plate, crisscross two anchovies on a whole pepper or a tomato slice. Serve with pepper mill, wine vinegar, olive oil for seasoning.

Makes 4 to 5 servings.

ANTIPASTO

Preparation Time: 4 minutes
Cooking Time: None

Salami slices, sardines, tuna, provolone or other cheese slices, olives, celery heart will make a delectable antipasto, designed to satisfy appetites while the pasta water is coming to a boil. Arrange these ingredients on a tray or set them out in bowls, adding red peppers, marinated mushrooms, Artichoke Hearts, Caponata (page 36) according to your taste or your supplies. Pass the pepper mill and the oil and vinegar. If the antipasto is generous enough, and you add crusty Italian bread, plus a bottle of dry wine, you'll have a thoroughly delightful meal even without the pasta course.

ARTICHOKE HEARTS A LA GRECQUE

Preparation Time: 3 minutes
Cooking Time: None

1 *can (8 ounces) artichokes*	*3 tablespoons oil*
in brine	*1 tablespoon vinegar*
1 *clove garlic, crushed,*	*Few grains pepper*
or dash garlic powder	*Pinch oregano*
¼ *teaspoon salt*	*Dash Tabasco*

Drain artichokes and place in bowl. Crush garlic with salt, add remaining ingredients. Pour over artichokes, stir gently to coat. Serve with picks.

1-Minute Shortcut: Arrange marinated artichoke hearts from a jar on plate. Add dash of Tabasco for extra zest.

ASPARAGUS ROLLS

Preparation Time: 3 minutes for 6 rolls
Cooking Time: 2 to 3 minutes

Spears of cooked or canned
asparagus, drained

White bread slices (cut in half
and with crusts removed)
Mayonnaise

Cut asparagus to width of bread pieces. Spread bread with mayonnaise. Place asparagus spear at one end and roll up. Brown in buttered skillet or in oven, seam side down. Serve warm.

AVOCADO AND GRAPEFRUIT

Preparation Time: 2 minutes
Cooking Time: None

1 *ripe avocado*
1 *can (8 ounces) grapefruit*
 sections

Salt
Tabasco
Lime or lemon wedges

Cut ripe avocado in half, remove seed and pile grapefruit sections in hollow. (If you have more time, peel avocado and cut into sections, arrange on platter alternatively with grapefruit sections.) Serve with salt, Tabasco, lime or lemon wedges. Season to taste, or pass French dressing spiked with a little grapefruit juice.

Makes 2 servings.

For Avocado Dip see Guacamole, page 40.

BRANDIED BLUE CHEESE CROCK

Preparation Time: 5 minutes
Cooking Time: None

6 ounces (¾ cup) blue
   cheese
6 ounces (¾ cup) butter

1 teaspoon prepared mustard
Pinch nutmeg
2 tablespoons brandy

Have cheese and butter at room temperature to soften. Mash together to blend well. Blend in seasonings and brandy. Serve with crackers as a spread.

Makes about 1½ cups.

BRANDIED LIVER PATE

Preparation Time: 6 minutes
Cooking Time: 10 minutes

3 tablespoons butter
½ pound chicken livers, cut in
   half
2 teaspoons cut onion
½ teaspoon salt

⅛ teaspoon pepper
1 tablespoon brandy
2 ounces cream cheese,
   softened
¼ cup chopped walnuts

Melt butter in a skillet and sauté chicken livers for about 5 minutes, stirring. Add onion, salt and pepper, and cook, stirring, 5 minutes more. Whirl mixture with brandy in blender, just until smooth, or chop finely. Combine with cream cheese. Stir in walnuts.

Yield: About 1 cup.

CAPONATA

Preparation Time: ½ minute
Cooking Time: None

Caponata—savory eggplant sautéed with diced red peppers, celery, capers, olives, tomatoes and onions—needs only be turned out of the small (and inexpensive) can. Serve with small forks or spoon onto crackers or endive leaves. Great as part of antipasto, too.

Serves 2; or 4 as part of antipasto.

CHEESE CHOICE

Preparation Time: 1 to 2 minutes
Cooking Time: None

A fine cheese, set on a plate or board, can be all the appetizer you need. Two kinds—one mild, one zesty, or one soft, one firm—are even better. Serve with crisp crackers or thin-sliced bread, or a loaf to cut as wanted. Or serve with apples or pears, or with radishes or nuts, to your taste. To do a fine cheese justice, serve it at room temperature rather than refrigerator-cold. And when you are down to bits and pieces of cheese, blend them into a cheese crock with butter and whiskey, beer or wine. Store this "bank" of satisfying flavor in the refrigerator and add to it at will.

CHEESE PUFFS

Preparation Time: 4 minutes
Cooking Time: 4 minutes

½ cup sharp cheese, cut in cubes
1 egg

1 green onion
Worcestershire Sauce
6 to 8 slices French bread

Place coarsely cut cheese in blender container or bowl with egg, cut-up onion, dash of Worcestershire sauce. Whirl to blend thoroughly; scrape down and repeat if necessary. Or mash and beat by hand. Pile onto French bread slices, spreading to edge. Broil about 3 minutes, until topping puffs and browns. Serve immediately.

Makes 3 to 4 servings.

CHOPPED LIVER SPREAD

Preparation Time: 7 minutes
Cooking Time: 7 minutes

½ pound liver, any kind	bacon dripping or butter
1 large onion, sliced	2 eggs
4 tablespoons chicken fat,	Salt, pepper

Trim any skin or tendons from liver; cut into small pieces. Simmer with onion in fat until almost cooked through, about 4 minutes. Break eggs into pan, scramble in yellow and white patches, cooking just until eggs are set. Place all in blender or bowl and whirl or chop until mixture is smooth. Season with salt and pepper and add more fat, if necessary, to make a spreadable paste. Serve with thin brown bread. Makes a good spread for celery stalks, green pepper wedges, radishes, cucumber slices, as well as crackers.

Dips

These are quick dips to stir up. They will keep for several days in the refrigerator.

CLAM AND CHEESE DIP

Preparation Time: 6 minutes
Cooking Time: None

1 can (7 ounces) minced
  clams
½ pound cream cheese,
  softened

½ cup sour cream
1 teaspoon lemon juice
Salt, pepper
Worcestershire Sauce

Drain clams, reserving 3 tablespoons clam broth. Add broth to cream cheese; beat until smooth. Add clams and remaining ingredients, adjusting seasoning to taste. Serve as a dip with crackers or chips.

Makes about 3 cups.

Diet Note: Use cottage cheese in place of cream cheese, buttermilk instead of sour cream. Serve with lettuce leaf or cucumber-slice dippers.

RED CAVIAR DIP

Preparation Time: 2 minutes
Cooking Time: None

1 jar (4 ounces) red caviar
½ pint sour cream

1 tablespoon chopped chives

Set out caviar with bowl of sour cream sprinkled with chives. Serve with chips, crackers or raw vegetables.

Makes 4 servings.

CUCUMBER AND SHRIMP

Preparation Time: 3 minutes
Cooking Time: None

Wash cucumber; do not peel. Run tines of fork down skin. Cut cucumber into thick slices. Top each slice with canned or cooked shrimp, or with smoked oysters or clams. Add a dab of mayonnaise, sprinkle with lemon juice.

CUMBERLAND FRANKS

Preparation Time: 5 minutes
Cooking Time: 6 minutes

1 *pound cocktail frankfurters*
½ *cup currant jelly*
½ *teaspoon prepared mustard*
¼ *cup orange juice, sherry or*
  whiskey

1 *slice unpeeled lemon,*
  minced
1 *slice onion, minced*

Heat cocktail frankfurters in water; drain. (Or use regular frankfurters cut into bite-sized chunks.) In serving pan melt jelly, add mustard, juice (or liquor), lemon and onion to make a chunky sauce. Add frankfurters and heat to warm through. Serve with picks.

Makes 8 servings.

DEVILED HAM PUFFS

Preparation Time: 4 to 5 minutes
Cooking Time: 2 minutes

1 *can (3 ounces) deviled ham*
  spread

2 *tablespoons mayonnaise*
½ *teaspoon prepared mustard*

Spread ham on rounds of firm bread or crackers. Combine mayonnaise and mustard. Spoon over ham, broil until topping is golden and puffed. Serve hot.

Makes 6 puffs.

GLAZED HAM BITES

Preparation Time: 4 minutes
Cooking Time: 2 minutes

Cut canned ham (or leftover cooked ham) into ½-inch cubes. Brush with prepared Chinese sweet-and-sour sauce, or duck sauce. Arrange on foil on baking sheet. Broil a few minutes to glaze. Serve with picks.

GUACAMOLE

Preparation Time: 5 minutes
Cooking Time: None

1 *ripe avocado*
⅛ *teaspoon crushed red pepper*
1 *lemon or lime, juiced*

Dash of salt
1 *tablespoon minced onion or shallot* (*optional*)

Cut avocado in half, remove seed, scrape pulp into bowl and mash with remaining ingredients. Serve as dip or spread, with corn chips or toasted tortillas.

Makes 2 to 4 servings.

HAM BATONS

Preparation Time: 4 minutes
Cooking Time: None

4 *tablespoons cream cheese*
1 *tablespoon sour cream*
1 *teaspoon horseradish*

Pinch of mustard
6 *thin slices boiled ham*

Beat cream cheese with sour cream and seasonings. Spread on ham slices; roll up. Cut in half to serve.

Makes 12 rolls.

HERBED "GERVAISE" CHEESE

Preparation Time: 5 minutes
Cooking Time: None

¼ cup heavy cream or yogurt
½ pound cottage cheese
1 tablespoon chopped chives
1 tablespoon chopped parsley
1 tablespoon fresh chopped tarragon or 1 teaspoon dried
1 tablespoon cracked black pepper

Place all ingredients except pepper in blender container and whirl smooth, or mash and blend well. Empty cheese mixture onto waxed paper or plastic. Form into round, then coat with cracked pepper.

MELON AND PROSCIUTTO

Preparation Time: 3 to 10 minutes (for 2 or 10)
Cooking Time: None

Peel and cut ripe honeydew or cantaloupe into thin wedges; wrap in thinly sliced prosciutto ham. Sprinkle with lemon juice, pass the pepper mill.

Variations: Use thin-sliced baked ham, salami, pastrami, dried beef or other salted meats; dieters use white meat of turkey. Or substitute fresh or dried figs, prunes or juicy pear wedges for the melon.

Nuts—Seasoned to Your Taste

These quickly toasted nuts have special flavor—good with after-dinner drinks, too.

TOASTED ALMONDS

Preparation Time: ½ minute
Cooking Time: 4 minutes

2 tablespoons butter
1 can (1 cup) blanched
  almonds

1 teaspoon seasoned salt

Melt butter; add almonds. Cook, stirring often, about 3 minutes, until nuts are golden brown. Sprinkle with seasoned salt and stir through. Serve warm or cold.

TOASTED PECANS OR WALNUTS

Preparation Time: ½ minute
Cooking Time: 4 minutes

2 tablespoons butter
2 tablespoons soy sauce

1 teaspoon sugar
2 cups pecan or walnut halves

Melt butter, add soy sauce and sugar. Cook for a minute or two. Add nuts and cook, stirring, until the nuts are crisp and amber. Serve warm or cold. Cooled nuts may be stored in an airtight container.

PORT WINE CHEDDAR

Preparation Time: 5 minutes
Cooking Time: None

½ pound ripe Cheddar
  cheese, shredded, or 2 cups
  combined cheeses to taste,
  shredded

¼ cup port (or more)
1 teaspoon caraway seeds

Have cheese soft at room temperature; mash well with remaining ingredients. Pack into a crock and serve at once; or cover, store in refrigerator until needed.

RADISHES AND BUTTER

Preparation Time: 1 to 2 minutes
Cooking Time: None

Radishes in season—red, white or black—make zesty appetizers. Trim most of stem from red radishes, but leave a bit of green stem for handle. Peel white radishes and cut lengthwise; peel black radishes and slice crosswise. Serve any of these with softened sweet butter and coarse salt.

SARDINE SPREAD

Preparation Time: 3 to 4 minutes
Cooking Time: None

1 can (3¾ ounces) skinless and boneless sardines
1 tablespoon mayonnaise
Juice of 1 lemon
Pepper, Tabasco

Mash sardines with their oil; beat in mayonnaise, lemon juice and seasonings with fork. Use as a spread on crackers or thin black bread. Handsome to serve heaped in emptied lemon shell, with thin slice cut from base so it will stand.
    Makes 1 to 4 servings.

SAUCY MUSHROOMS

Preparation Time: 3 minutes
Cooking Time: None

1 can (1 pound) whole mushrooms
2 tablespoons lemon juice
4 tablespoons olive oil
1 garlic clove, mashed
Salt, pepper

Drain mushrooms. Cover with mixture of remaining ingredients. Serve at room temperature or chill until serving time. Keeps well in refrigerator.

SHRIMP IN WINE

Preparation Time: 6 minutes
Cooking Time: 7 minutes

1 *pound fresh or frozen*
  shrimp, peeled and deveined
Juice of 1 *lime or lemon*
1 *teaspoon salt*
3 *tablespoons oil*
1 *onion, sliced thin*

2 *cloves garlic*
¼ *cup white wine*
1 *tablespoon (about) soy*
  sauce
Chopped parsley or tarragon

Sprinkle shrimp with lime or lemon juice and salt. Heat oil in skillet; sauté onion and garlic until onion is transparent. Discard garlic, reserve onion slices. Drain shrimp, reserving marinade. Cook shrimp in flavored oil for 3 minutes, stirring occasionally, until they are just pink. Add wine, soy sauce and marinade; cook, stirring shrimp, to heat sauce a few minutes. Arrange shrimp and onion in bowl. Sprinkle with chopped parsley or tarragon. Serve warm or chill before serving.

Variation: Cut fish fillets into strips and prepare as above.

TOMATO AU BLEU

Preparation Time: 2 minutes
Cooking Time: None

Cut ripe beefsteak tomato into thick slices; sprinkle each slice with crumbled blue cheese. Serve with sour cream, or oil and vinegar.

VEGETABLE CRUDITES

Preparation Time: 3 to 6 minutes
Cooking Time: None

Arrange cleaned, cut raw vegetables on a platter or in a bowl of shaved ice. Center with a bowl of sour cream or mayonnaise seasoned with curry powder or with a dip of your choice (page 38). Imbed in ice your choice of: raw asparagus (break off tough ends, which snap at the tender point, wash tops), cucumber sticks, raw mushrooms wiped clean, broccoli flowerets, carrot sticks, cauliflower buds, celery sticks, young green beans, green pepper strips, trimmed green onions, young zucchini sticks. Dip vegetables in sauce to taste.

4 *Superspecial Soups*

On a busy day, a soup-bowl supper is restoring and relaxing, to prepare as well as to eat. What's more, soup is economical and infinitely varied in its ways.

The recipes given here begin with what you have on hand and turn out flavorful, nourishing soups in short order. The liquid may be water, or broth (instant or home-cooked or canned stock), tomato juice, milk, or liquors of vegetables or fruits that you have saved and stored in the refrigerator. The solids may be leftover vegetables, toast, cereal, rice, pastas—your own version of the peasant "stone soup" in the Russian fairy tale, which started with a stone and water and then with the addition of a carrot, a potato, a few leaves of cabbage, a spoonful of barley or beans, became a savory supper.

Homemade stock is the base of the greatest soups, but very creditable and nourishing soups may be made with improvised or commercial beginnings.

Build on canned or packaged soup bases, too, adding leftover vegetables, bits of meat, rice, last night's salad put through the blender, to produce flavorful bowls of soup. Serve with hot bread, salad, cheese and fruit and you will have a thoroughly satisfying meal.

For a satisfying supper in a bowl, take your pick of the hearty soups that follow.

BLACK BEAN SOUP

Preparation Time: 10 minutes
Cooking Time: 15 minutes

1 tablespoon oil
1 onion, chopped
1 carrot, chopped
1 stalk celery, chopped
1 can (1 pound) black beans
1 pint broth or consommé
3 sprigs parsley
1 slice cooked ham, slivered
Pinch of cloves

Pinches of thyme and mace or
   allspice
½ teaspoon dry mustard
Salt, pepper
1 teaspoon Worcestershire
   sauce
¼ cup sherry
Lemon slices or sour cream

Heat oil in soup pot, add onions, carrots and celery, and cook briefly, stirring, until vegetables are glazed. Add beans, consommé, parsley, ham and remaining ingredients except lemon slices. Bring to a boil and simmer to heat. If desired, purée or whirl in blender. Garnish each serving with a lemon slice or spoon of sour cream.

Makes 3 to 4 servings.

BORSCHT

Preparation Time: 4 to 5 minutes
Cooking Time: 16 minutes

4 small new potatoes
   (optional)
1 can (1 pound) sliced beets
1½ cups beef broth (home-
   made, canned or instant)

3 tablespoons lemon juice
2 tablespoons sugar
Salt, pepper
1 egg
½ cup sour cream

Wash new potatoes, halve and boil in salted water to cover until tender, while soup is being prepared. Purée beets with a little of their liquor in blender, or chop. Pour into soup pot, add

remaining liquor and beef broth; simmer 5 minutes. Add lemon juice and seasonings; stir to dissolve sugar. Remove from heat. Beat egg with a little hot liquid and stir into soup. Slip skins from potatoes. Serve with a hot boiled potato in each plate, and top with sour cream. Leftover borscht is very good cold, too.
Makes 4 servings.

CHEDDAR CHEESE SOUP

Preparation Time: 7 minutes
Cooking Time: 12 minutes

2 tablespoons butter
2 tablespoons flour
2 cups milk
1 teaspoon salt
½ teaspoon prepared mustard

Pinch of cayenne
½ cup boiling water
1 bouillon cube
2½ cups grated Cheddar
cheese

Melt butter, stir in flour and cook for a moment without browning. Gradually stir in milk and cook, stirring until sauce is thickened and smooth. Add seasonings. Add the boiling water and the bouillon cube and stir until the cube melts; add the cheese, mix and heat through. Serve with toasted herb bread.
Makes 4 servings.

SPANISH CHICK-PEA AND SAUSAGE SOUP

Preparation Time: 5 minutes
Cooking Time: 15 minutes

2 cups canned chick-peas (or
other beans)
2 cups beef broth
¼ cup white wine
1 clove garlic, minced
Pinch of dried red pepper,
crushed

½ teaspoon sofrito (or chili
powder)
4 ounces Spanish sausage or
Italian hard salami, thinly
sliced

Drain peas or beans. Combine with broth, wine, garlic season-ings. Stir in sausage or salami slices and heat gently, stirring often, for about 15 minutes. Garnish with a spoonful of sour cream, and shredded lettuce or avocado slices.

Makes 2 hearty main-dish servings.

Note: For a smooth soup, purée peas or beans in blender, 1 cup at a time, adding ½ cup of broth to each cup, at start of preparation.

CHRYSANTHEMUM POT

Preparation Time: 15 minutes
Cooking Time: At the table

Bring 1 to 1½ quarts chicken broth to boil in chafing dish or Chinese "chrysanthemum pot" or fondue pot. Surround with thin strips of raw chicken, fish, veal, mushroom slices, scallions and watercress or spinach. Have at hand small bowls of soy sauce and grated horseradish spiked with ginger and mustard for dip-ping after foods are cooked. For each diner, provide chopsticks or fondue forks to hold chosen food in simmering broth a few minutes until cooked. After meat and vegetables are seasoned to taste and eaten, serve broth in small bowls, with cooked rice, if desired.

CLAM BISQUE

Preparation Time: 2 minutes
Cooking Time: 6 minutes

1 *can* (10 *ounces*) *minced clams*	1 *tablespoon lemon juice*
1 *cup chicken broth*	2 *egg yolks*
2 *tablespoons butter*	1 *cup cream*
	Paprika

Heat together juice from clams, broth, butter and lemon juice. Add clams. Beat egg yolks with a fork, warm with a little hot liquid and return to pan, stirring well. Add cream and heat gently.

Serve at once, sprinkled with paprika. Makes 3 servings.

CLAM CHOWDER (MANHATTAN)

Preparation Time: 10 minutes
Cooking Time: 15 minutes

2 potatoes
2 tablespoons butter
2 onions, chopped
1 green pepper
2 stalks celery
1 quart boiling water
1 can (1 pound) tomatoes

1 can (10 ounces) minced clams
1 can (10 ounces) whole clams
¼ teaspoon thyme
Salt, pepper

Peel and dice potatoes; glaze in butter. Dice onions and add; then dice pepper and celery and add. Stir until glazed, about 4 minutes. Add boiling water, tomatoes, liquid drained from the clams, and thyme. Simmer about 10 minutes, until potatoes are tender. Add clams, heat briefly and season with salt and pepper.

Makes 6 servings.

CLAM CHOWDER (NEW ENGLAND)

Preparation Time: 6 minutes
Cooking Time: 24 minutes

2 strips bacon or salt pork, minced
2 large potatoes
1 small onion
2 cups water
½ teaspoon salt
⅛ teaspoon pepper

2 cups milk
1 tablespoon butter
1 can (10 ounces) minced clams
6 soda crackers
Red pepper sauce

Render salt pork or bacon pieces in soup pot. Peel potatoes, cut into half-inch cubes and drop into bowl of cold water. Dice onion. Add onion to pot. Drain potatoes and add. Cook until glazed but not brown. Add water, salt, pepper, and boil 10 minutes, until potatoes are almost tender. Add milk, butter; heat, then add clams and their liquor, and soda crackers, crumbled. Cook gently until potatoes are tender and soup thickened, about 3 minutes more. Adjust seasoning, add a few drops of red pepper sauce.

Makes 4 servings.

ESCAROLE SOUP

Preparation Time: 6 minutes
Cooking Time: 19 minutes

1½ quarts chicken broth
¼ pound fine noodles
Salt, pepper
1 small head escarole

3 eggs
4 tablespoons grated Parmesan cheese

Bring broth to boil, add noodles, salt and pepper. Shred escarole and add to pot. When noodles are tender, beat eggs with cheese and add gradually, beating constantly. Heat until egg sets, about 3 minutes. Serve immediately.

Makes 4 to 6 servings.

FISH CHOWDER, NEW ENGLAND

Preparation Time: 8 minutes
Cooking Time: 17 minutes

2 tablespoons butter
1 onion, sliced thin
1 pound fish fillets (cod, haddock, other)
1 cup thin-sliced potatoes
1 teaspoon salt

Water
1 tablespoon butter
1 tablespoon flour
2 cups milk
Pepper
2 tablespoons minced parsley

Melt butter in a large pot and cook onion until golden. Cube fish fillets and add to pot with potatoes. Add salt and water barely to cover and simmer gently about 10 minutes, until the potatoes are just cooked through. Meanwhile, blend butter with flour with a fork. Add this thickening mixture to the pot, bit by bit, stirring carefully. Add milk and pepper, simmer 5 minutes but do not boil. Add parsley.

Makes 4 servings.

FRENCH ONION SOUP

Preparation Time: 5 minutes
Cooking Time: 10 to 12 minutes

4 onions, sliced thin
2 tablespoons butter
4 cups hot water
4 bouillon cubes
1 teaspoon Worcestershire
  sauce

¼ pound Gruyère cheese,
  slivered
French bread, toasted
¼ cup grated Parmesan cheese

In saucepan, cook onions in butter very slowly, until tender, translucent, and on the verge of turning golden. Add water, bouillon cubes, Worcestershire sauce; bring to boil and simmer for a few minutes. Divide Gruyère cheese into heatproof bowls, add soup, top soup with toast and then with grated Parmesan, and put under the broiler for a moment, if desired, to melt the cheese a bit.

Makes 4 servings.

GAZPACHO

Preparation Time: 12 minutes
Cooking Time: None

1 bouillon cube
¼ cup hot water
2 ice cubes
1 clove garlic
1 medium onion, cut
3 tomatoes, peeled and cut up
1 green pepper, seeded, cut
½ teaspoon Worcestershire
   sauce

¼ cup lemon juice
¼ cup oil
1¼ cups chilled tomato juice
⅛ teaspoon cayenne pepper
¼ teaspoon white pepper
Salt
Slivers of ham, cucumber,
   sausage, cheese, for garnish

Dissolve bouillon cube in hot water, then add ice cubes to chill. Put remaining ingredients, except garnish, into blender and purée. Add bouillon. Garnish with strips of ham, cucumber, sausage, cheese.
   Makes 4 servings.

GREEN PEA SOUP WITH FRANKFURTERS

Preparation Time: 3 to 6 minutes
Cooking Time: 9 minutes

1 can (16 ounces) green peas
1 pint broth

Pinch of mustard
2 to 4 frankfurters

Whirl green peas with their liquid in blender to purée. Stir in broth and mustard. Bring to boil. Add sliced frankfurters. Heat through.
   Makes 4 servings.

MEATBALL SOUP

Preparation Time: 12 minutes
Cooking Time: 12 minutes

½ pound ground chuck
1 tablespoon minced onion
¼ cup milk
¼ cup oats
½ teaspoon salt

¼ teaspoon pepper
¼ teaspoon tarragon
Flour
2 tablespoons butter

Combine meat, onion, milk, oats and seasonings. Shape 12 small balls, roll in flour, brown in butter. Add to prepared French Onion Soup (page 52) omitting Gruyère cheese and toast. Simmer until soup is slightly thickened. Serve with grated Parmesan, if desired.
Makes 4 servings.

MINESTRONE

Preparation Time: 6 minutes
Cooking Time: 24 minutes

4 strips bacon
1 onion
1 clove garlic
1 package (9 ounces) frozen
   mixed vegetables
2 quarts water
4 bouillon cubes
1 can (about 1 pound)
   tomatoes

1 celery stalk, slivered
2 sprigs parsley, minced
Pinch of oregano
Salt, pepper
½ cup elbow macaroni
Parmesan cheese (optional)

Sauté bacon in soup kettle. Add onion, garlic. Add mixed vegetables, water, bouillon cubes, tomatoes, celery, parsley, oregano and seasonings. Bring to a boil, add macaroni; cook about 15 minutes. Pass Parmesan cheese to add to soup, if desired.
Makes 8 servings; keeps and reheats well.

MUSHROOM SOUP EPICURE

Preparation Time: 10 minutes
Cooking Time: 12 minutes

2 tablespoons butter
2 tablespoons flour
3 cups chicken bouillon
1½ cups mushrooms

1 cup cream
2 or 3 hard-cooked eggs,
chopped

Melt butter, stir in flour and cook for a moment, still stirring. Add bouillon and cook, stirring constantly, until the soup is smooth and thickened. Simmer 5 minutes. Wipe mushrooms clean. Cut up and put into blender container with a small amount of the soup, and purée. Add to the soup. Add the cream, heat, and simmer 3 to 4 minutes. Top with chopped hard-cooked eggs. Good hot or iced.

Makes 6 servings.

OYSTER STEW

Preparation Time: 2 minutes
Cooking Time: 5 to 8 minutes

¼ cup butter
2 cups oysters, fresh or canned
1½ cups milk
½ cup cream

½ teaspoon salt
⅛ teaspoon pepper
⅛ teaspoon paprika
2 tablespoons chopped parsley

Melt butter in pan over very low heat. Add raw oysters and their liquor and bring just to the boiling point. Add milk, cream, salt and pepper; heat slowly until oysters rise to surface. (If you use canned oysters, add them with the milk and seasonings, heat all together.) Sprinkle with paprika and parsley.

Makes 2 servings.

PASTA E FAGIOLI

Preparation Time: 11 minutes
Cooking Time: 8 minutes

2 cups beef broth
1 rib celery, diced
1 small carrot, finely diced
1 small onion, chopped
2 teaspoons parsley, chopped
1 can (about 1 pound) red
   kidney beans

2 tablespoons olive oil
Salt and pepper
1 handful of ditalini (or elbow
   macaroni)
Cheese for garnish

Bring broth to boil. Meanwhile, prepare vegetables and parsley and add to boiling broth. Drain beans, mash half and add to pot; add remaining beans whole. Add olive oil and season generously with salt and pepper. Add ditalini to boiling soup. When soup returns to boil, reduce heat and cook just until ditalini are tender, about 8 minutes. Spoon immediately into large soup bowls. Garnish with grated Romano or Parmesan cheese.
   Makes 2 hearty main-dish servings.

POTATO SOUP

Preparation Time: 10 minutes
Cooking Time: 20 minutes

2 cups water or chicken broth
2 tablespoons butter
2 thin-sliced leeks or large
   scallions, whites only, sliced
1 onion, sliced
2 potatoes, peeled and thinly
   diced

Salt
2 cups milk
Pepper
1 cup cream
Chopped chives for garnish

Set water or broth to boil. Melt butter in saucepan, cook leeks or scallions and onion until transparent, but not browned. Add potatoes, water or broth, salt. Boil until potatoes are tender, about 10 minutes. If desired, put through a food mill or purée in blender. Add milk and heat slowly to a boil, stirring often. Adjust seasoning with pepper. Add cream and heat through. Serve topped with chopped chives.

Makes 6 servings.

Also see Vichyssoise (page 60).

QUICK PEA OR ASPARAGUS SOUP

Preparation Time: 4 minutes
Cooking Time: 4 to 5 minutes

1 can (16 ounces) *asparagus or* | 1 can (10½ ounces) *condensed*
small peas | *consommé*
2 tablespoons *butter* | 2 slices *boiled ham, cut in*
1 small *onion, diced* | *slivers*

Place asparagus or peas, with liquor, in blender container and blend smooth. Heat butter and onion in soup pot. Add blended vegetables and consommé, bring to a boil, add slivered ham to heat through.

Makes 4 servings.

SPINACH VELVET SOUP

Preparation Time: 3 minutes
Cooking Time: 8 minutes

2 tablespoons *butter* | 2½ cups *milk*
1 scallion *or small onion,* | 2 *bouillon cubes*
minced | Salt, pepper
1 tablespoon *flour* | Dash of *nutmeg*
1 cup *cooked spinach* | Semisoft *cheese slivers*

Melt butter, cook onion for a few minutes. Stir in flour and cook until smooth. Place in blender container with spinach and 1 cup milk. Blend smooth. Put into soup pot. Add remaining milk and bouillon cubes and cook, stirring, until the soup is thickened and smooth. Season with salt, pepper and a dash of nutmeg. Top with cheese slivers.

Makes 4 servings.

STRACIATELLA ALLA ROMANA (ROMAN EGG-DROP SOUP)

Preparation Time: 3 minutes
Cooking Time: 9 minutes

1½ quarts chicken broth
3 eggs
3½ tablespoons grated
  Parmesan cheese

1 tablespoon chopped parsley

Bring broth to boil. Beat eggs, cheese and parsley together (or whirl in blender). Gradually add egg mixture to broth, stirring constantly with a fork or slotted wooden spoon to prevent lumping. Simmer until egg strands are set, about 3 minutes. Serve hot.

Makes 6 servings.

SWEET-SOUR CABBAGE SOUP

Preparation Time: 10 minutes (overlaps cooking)
Cooking Time: 25 minutes

1 can (1 pound) sauerkraut,
  drained
1 can (1 pound) stewed
  tomatoes
1 can (8 ounces) tomato sauce
¼ cup light-brown sugar
1 tablespoon lemon juice
1½ cups water

1 tart apple, peeled and diced
1 small box (1½ ounces)
  seedless raisins
½ pound ground chuck
1 egg
¼ cup precooked rice
¼ teaspoon salt

Combine sauerkraut, tomatoes, tomato sauce, sugar, lemon juice, water, apple and raisins. Cover, bring to boil. Meanwhile, combine chuck with egg, rice and salt. Shape into small balls. Lay on top of sauerkraut. Cook 15 to 20 minutes.

Makes 6 servings.

SWISS SOUP

Preparation Time: 4 minutes
Cooking Time: 7 minutes

4 slices toasted bread
8 tablespoons grated Swiss
  cheese

2 cups boiling-hot milk
2 tablespoons browned butter
Salt, pepper, nutmeg

Put a slice of bread in the bottom of each of 2 soup plates and top with half the grated cheese, second slice of bread. Add 1 cup milk to each serving, cover the plate and let stand for a few minutes in a warm place. Top each with half the browned butter and season to taste.

Serves 2.

TOMATO-CRAB BISQUE

Preparation Time: 3 minutes
Cooking Time: 8 minutes

1 can (10¾ ounces) tomato
  soup
1¼ cups milk

1 can (about 6½ ounces) crab
  meat, drained
Tabasco to taste

Heat soup and milk, stirring constantly. Add crab meat and Tabasco, heat through, stirring.

Makes 2 to 3 servings.

VICHYSSOISE

Preparation Time: 4 minutes
Cooking Time: 6 minutes

2 *leeks or large scallions*
1 *medium onion*
1 *tablespoon butter*
2 *cups boiling water or broth*
½ *cup instant potatoes*

Salt, pepper
1 *cup milk*
1 *cup cream, heavy or light as*
preferred
Chopped chives

Cut white parts of leeks or scallions and onion. Melt butter in saucepan. Add onion and leeks; cook until soft but not brown. Place in blender container with 1 cup boiling water or broth, and whirl smooth. Return to saucepan, add potatoes and remaining water or broth, stir smooth. Remove from heat. Stir in cold milk, then cream. If desired, chill. Serve with a sprinkling of chopped chives on each portion.

Makes 6 servings.

Note: If there isn't time to refrigerate this, you will enjoy Vichyssoise as Louis Diat, its "inventor," recalled having it in his childhood—hot potato and leek soup cooled with a ladleful of cream from the milkmaid's pail, as he sat on his doorstep in Vichy.

ZUPPA PAVESE

Preparation Time: 4 minutes
Cooking Time: 7 minutes

2 *cups chicken broth*
2 *eggs*

1 *cup shredded escarole or*
lettuce
Parmesan cheese, grated

Bring broth to a boil in a shallow pan. Break an egg into a saucer. With a spoon stir the broth to make a vortex; slip the egg into the center of the vortex and poach just until the white is set. Remove with a slotted spoon to a soup bowl. Repeat to poach next egg. Add escarole and cook 1 minute. Cover eggs in bowls with soup. Serve with grated cheese and buttered, toasted French bread. Simply beautiful.

Serves 2.

5 *International Skillet Meals*

The skillet is the most universal pot of all—the one pan to buy if there is only one pan to buy. Because it is shallow, the skillet or frying pan heats quickly over a broad area.

"Cut it thin and cook it fast" is the motto of the skillet cook. Start with thinly cut pieces of meat or poultry, fish or vegetables. After several of these favorites, you'll discover that the procedure for a wide variety of specialties is essentially the same. Heat fat or liquid in the skillet and first cook the protein portion quickly. This sears the meat or fish and prevents loss of juices. Then the other ingredients and typical national flavorings are added, and the whole cooked over gentle heat, just long enough to produce tender meat and crisp vegetables with all their natural flavor. Where cereal or rice is the base, proceed according to individual recipes.

The particular meats, fish, poultry or other main-dish ingredient you choose will shift with your market supply. Or you may want to substitute hard-cooked eggs or even soybean curd for the meat or fish. The method remains the same. It is the saucing and seasonings that make the distinctive flavor in the ethnic favorites which follow.

BEEF OR LAMB STROGANOFF

Preparation Time: 12 minutes
Cooking Time: 12 minutes

1 *pound beef sirloin or lamb*
 steak
Salt, pepper, paprika
2 *tablespoons oil*

2 *tablespoons butter*
½ *small onion, chopped*
¼ *pound mushrooms, sliced*
1 *cup commercial sour cream*

Cut meat into thin, uniform strips across the grain. Season. Heat oil in a skillet. Add meat, cook quickly until browned, turning to cook evenly. Push meat to side of pan. In center add butter, onion and mushrooms. Cook, stirring until browned. Add sour cream. Stir through and heat gently. Adjust seasoning if necessary. Serve with rice or noodles.

Makes 4 servings.

CHICKEN 'N' RICE CREOLE

Preparation Time: 5 minutes
Cooking Time: 25 minutes

¼ *cup oil*
2 *pounds chicken wings*
1 *onion, chopped*
1 *small green pepper, diced*

1 *jar* (1 *pound*) *spaghetti*
 sauce
Pinch of thyme
2 *cups quick-cooking rice*

Heat oil in large, deep skillet. Brown chicken wings well. Add onion and green pepper to pan toward end of browning (about 10 minutes). Cook until soft. Stir in spaghetti sauce, add thyme, bring to boil. Push wings to side of pan, add rice, stir, and arrange chicken wings on top. Cover, cook about 5 minutes longer, until rice is tender and liquid almost absorbed.

Makes 4 servings.

CHINESE FISH WITH VEGETABLES

Preparation Time: 6 minutes
Cooking Time: 6 minutes

½ pound fish fillets, cut into strips
1 tablespoon cornstarch
½ teaspoon salt
Dash of red pepper
3 tablespoons oil
Small piece of fresh ginger root, diced (keep in the freezer, to cut as needed)
2 scallions, trimmed and cut into 2-inch sections

1 package (9 ounces) frozen Chinese vegetables, thawed
1 ripe tomato, cut into sixths
3 tablespoons broth
1 tablespoon soy sauce
1 tablespoon sherry
1 teaspoon sugar
1 teaspoon vinegar
1 tablespoon cornstarch
1 tablespoon water
2 cups cooked rice

Cut fish (or chicken, pork or *tofu*) into thin strips. Coat with cornstarch, salt, pepper. Let stand a few minutes while other ingredients are assembled. Heat oil in skillet. Toss fish strips to glaze quickly. Add diced ginger root, scallions, Chinese vegetables, tomato. Stir to glaze. Add broth, boil a minute or two. Add soy sauce, sherry, sugar, vinegar, cornstarch stirred with water. Bring to boil, stirring, until thickened and clear. Serve over cooked rice. Vegetarians make this with bean curd (*tofu*). Good!

Makes 2 to 3 servings.

CHINESE FRIED RICE (CHOW FON)

Preparation Time: 6 minutes
Cooking Time: 8 minutes

2 scallions, chopped
3 tablespoons oil
2 cups cool cooked rice
¾ cup chopped fresh raw shrimp, or 1 can, about 7 ounces

1 tablespoon soy sauce
2 eggs, lightly beaten
Scallion for garnish

Cook chopped scallions gently in hot oil, add rice and shrimp and cook, stirring, until rice is hot and shrimp are pink. Add soy sauce and eggs, cook and stir until eggs are set. Garnish with another scallion, cut into slivers.

Makes 2 servings.

Variations: Instead of shrimp, use about 1 cup of diced left-over roast pork or ham or other cooked meat; or use cooked chicken; or a combination of meats. Or, add ½ cup well-drained bean sprouts or water chestnuts to mixture; omit scallion garnish and use slivered almonds or chopped cashews instead.

CHINESE PEPPER STEAK

Preparation Time: 7 minutes
Cooking Time: 9 minutes

1 pound tender chuck or round
 steak
¼ cup hot oil
1 garlic clove, minced
3 green peppers, cut in squares
2 peeled tomatoes, coarsely cut

1 onion, minced
2 to 4 tablespoons soy sauce
½ teaspoon sugar
1 tablespoon cornstarch
½ cup water or bouillon

Slice meat in thin diagonal strips. Brown strips in hot oil with garlic. Move meat and garlic to side of pan or to a separate dish. Add green peppers, tomatoes and onion to pan. Cook, stirring, until onion is transparent. Return meat to pan (if you have removed it) and add soy sauce and sugar. Stir in corn-starch blended with water or bouillon. Cook, stirring, until sauce is clear. Serve with rice.

Serves 4.

CHOUCROUTE GARNI

Preparation Time: 5 minutes
Cooking Time: 25 minutes

1 *pound cooked ham in thick slice*
1 *clove garlic*
1 *onion, diced*
1 *apple, diced*

1 *bay leaf*
1 *cup white wine*
1 *package* (2 *pounds*) *fresh sauerkraut*
4 *frankfurters, cut up*

Trim the fat from the ham slice and fry in a deep skillet; add garlic, onion and apple, cook until onion is golden. Add bay leaf and wine and simmer. Meanwhile, rinse sauerkraut under running cold water, drain, add to skillet. Top with ham, cut into serving pieces, and frankfurters. Cover pan, simmer over moderate heat until kraut is tender-crisp and most of liquid is absorbed.

Makes 6 to 8 servings.

CURRIED LAMB CHOPS

Preparation Time: 5 minutes
Cooking Time: 20 minutes

4 *shoulder lamb chops*
Salt, pepper
2 *tablespoons butter*
1 *teaspoon curry powder*
1 *onion, chopped*
2 *stalks celery and leaves, chopped*

1 *tart apple, chopped*
2 *tablespoons flour*
1 *cup boiling water*
1 *bouillon cube*

Season chops with salt and pepper and brown on both sides in skillet. Stack to side of pan. Melt butter, add curry powder and stir for a minute or two. Add onion, celery and apple to skillet, cook a minute longer. Sprinkle with flour, stir. Add water and bouillon cube and continue to cook, stirring, until sauce is thickened and smooth. Adjust seasoning with salt, pepper, and more curry, if desired. Replace chops in sauce, spooning sauce over; cover, simmer about 5 minutes. Serve with plain boiled rice and dishes of chutney, salted peanuts, chopped cucumber.

Makes 4 servings.

FRITTO MISTO

Preparation Time: 5 to 10 minutes
Cooking Time: 10 to 15 minutes

Eggplant   *Mushrooms*
Zucchini   *Artichoke hearts*
Cauliflower   *Veal*
Green pepper   *Chicken liver*
Onion   *Beef liver*

BATTER

1 *cup flour*   ¾ *cup water*
¼ *teaspoon salt*   1 *tablespoon olive oil*
1 *egg, separated*   *Oil for frying*

Choose any desired assortment of vegetables and meat; cut into thin, bite-sized slices or morsels. Arrange on a platter.

Make the batter: Mix flour and salt, add egg yolk, water and olive oil, whisk smooth. Beat the egg white stiff, fold in.

Heat oil (at depth of 3 inches) to moderate (365°F. on the deep-fat thermometer) at the table in an electric skillet, if possible. Dip pieces of vegetable and meat into the batter with a fork, drain excess, and fry until brown. Drain on paper toweling and serve at once. If necessary, fry the *fritto misto* in the kitchen and keep it warm in a slow oven (200°F.) until all pieces are ready to serve.

Makes 2 to 3 servings.

Also see Tempura, page 72.

HAM, YAMS AND APPLES

Preparation Time: 5 minutes
Cooking Time: 15 minutes

2 tablespoons butter
1 slice (about 1 pound)
   cooked ham
1 can (1 pound) sweet potatoes, drained

2 apples, sliced thin
¼ cup brown sugar
2 tablespoons orange juice

Melt butter in a large skillet; brown ham slice on one side. Turn. Arrange potatoes and apples around ham. Sprinkle with brown sugar and orange juice. Cook, covered, until bottom of ham slice is browned. Spoon juices over all.
   Makes 4 servings.

LAMB AND GREEN BEANS

Preparation Time: 12 minutes
Cooking Time: 13 minutes

½ pound lamb shoulder, cut
   in strips
2 tablespoons oil
1 medium onion, chopped
1 cup green beans, raw or
   frozen
1 medium green pepper, sliced

1 cup sliced celery
4 teaspoons cornstarch
1 tablespoon soy sauce
¾ cup liquid (juice from
   mushrooms and water)
Salt and pepper
1 can (4 ounces) mushrooms

Brown meat in hot oil in large heavy skillet. Add next 4 ingredients and cook 3 to 5 minutes. (You want the vegetables to be crisp.) Combine cornstarch, soy sauce, liquid and seasonings; add to skillet, stirring to mix thoroughly. Add mushrooms. Cook, stirring, until sauce is thickened and clear.
   Makes 4 servings.

MEATBALL STEW

Preparation Time: 8 minutes
Cooking Time: 22 minutes

1 egg
½ cup water
½ cup bread crumbs
1½ teaspoons salt
¼ teaspoon pepper
⅛ teaspoon ground clove
1 pound ground chuck or
    round
2 tablespoons oil
1 clove garlic

½ teaspoon salt
½ cup chopped onion
4 carrots, cut in slices
1 can (16 ounces) tomatoes,
    strained
½ cup water
1 package (9 ounces) frozen
    green beans, defrosted
1 can (12 ounces) corn ker-
    nels, drained

Beat the egg in a large bowl; add the water, crumbs, salt, pepper, clove. Add meat and stir with a fork until well mixed. Moisten hands, form meat mixture into small balls about 1½ inches in diameter. Heat the oil in a heavy pan or Dutch oven, brown meatballs in this. Crush garlic and salt together to make a paste. Add with the onion and carrots to the pan. Add tomatoes and water, bring to boil, stir in beans. Cover and cook for 15 minutes, shaking occasionally. Add the corn for the last 5 minutes to heat through.

Makes 4 to 6 servings.

MEXICAN PORK SKILLET

Preparation Time: 5 minutes
Cooking Time: 25 minutes

2 tablespoons fat
2 pounds pork loin or shoul-
    der, sliced thin
1 clove garlic, bruised
1 tablespoon lemon juice

¾ cup orange juice
½ teaspoon sugar
½ tablespoon Worcestershire
    sauce
Salt, pepper

Heat fat. Brown pork slices with garlic slowly over moderate heat. Remove and discard garlic. Add remaining ingredients. Simmer, covered, until sauce is thickened and pork is tender, about 20 minutes. Season to taste with salt and pepper.

Makes 6 to 8 servings.

SHRIMP MARINARA WITH PASTA SHELLS

Preparation Time: 8 minutes
Cooking Time: 12 minutes

2 quarts water
½ teaspoon salt
½ pound enriched macaroni
  shells (small or medium)
1 tablespoon oil
2 scallions, sliced (or ½
  onion, diced)

1 pound frozen shrimp, shelled
  and deveined
1 pint jar marinara sauce
Chopped basil or parsley
Grated Parmesan cheese

Set water with salt to boil, add macaroni shells and cook *al dente*. Meanwhile, heat oil in skillet, add scallions, then shrimp (or other seafood). Stir a minute or two to glaze, then add marinara sauce and heat through. Drain macaroni shells, top with seafood and sauce. Sprinkle with basil or parsley. Serve with grated Parmesan cheese.

Makes 4 servings.

Variation: Frozen fish fillets, cut in strips, can substitute for shrimp.

QUICK PAELLA VALENCIANA

Preparation Time: 10 minutes
Cooking Time: 18 minutes

2 *whole boned chicken breasts*
Salt, pepper
¼ *cup oil*
2 *cloves garlic, slivered*
1 *green pepper, chopped*
2 *onions, chopped*
2 *tablespoons snipped parsley*
½ *teaspoon oregano*

1 *can (about 1 pound) whole clams*
¼ *teaspoon saffron threads*
1½ *cups precooked converted rice*
½ *pound frozen shrimp, pre-cleaned*

Cut chicken breasts into 8 pieces. Season with salt and pepper. Heat oil in a deep skillet; brown chicken on all sides with garlic, pepper and onion. Add parsley and oregano to the skillet. Add the juice from the clams, plus water to make 1½ cups. Add saffron. Bring to a boil, add rice, stir. Cover skillet and cook 5 minutes, until rice is cooked thoroughly and liquid almost absorbed. Add shrimp, cook 2 minutes; add clams, heat through. Adjust seasoning with salt and pepper if necessary.

Makes 4 servings.

SUKIYAKI

Preparation Time: 12 minutes
Cooking Time: 11 minutes

1 *pound sliced top sirloin or round or chuck fillet*
1 *large onion*
3 *celery stalks*
¼ *pound mushrooms*
6 *scallions*
1 *can (5 ounces) water chest-nuts, drained*

oil for frying
½ *cup soy sauce*
¾ *cup beef bouillon*
¼ *cup sherry*
1 *tablespoon sugar*
¼ *pound spinach*

Cut beef in uniform thin strips across the grain; slice vegetables in thin diagonal strips. Arrange on a platter until serving time. Brown meat quickly in hot oil in skillet; push to side. Add remaining ingredients except spinach, cover pan, and cook 5 minutes. Add spinach, cover pan and cook 3 minutes longer. Stir and serve with boiled rice.

Makes 6 servings.

TEMPURA

Preparation Time: 10 minutes
Cooking Time: 18 minutes

1 *pound shrimp, shelled and precleaned*
1 *sweet potato, in ¼-inch slices*

1 *green pepper, in strips*
Oil for deep-frying

BATTER

1 *egg*
pinch of baking soda

2 *cups water*
1¾ *cups flour*

Arrange shrimp and vegetables in piles on a platter. Bring oil (at depth of 3 inches) to moderately hot temperature in a deep skillet or casserole; or use an automatic fryer, with the temperature set at 375° F.

Make the batter: Beat egg lightly, add baking soda dissolved in water. Add flour all at once and stir with a fork. The batter may be slightly lumpy. It should be thin and runny; add more water if necessary.

Using chopsticks or tongs, dip shrimp and vegetables into the batter, one piece at a time, then fry until golden. Drain on paper toweling. Eat at once, with dipping sauce of soy sauce, grating of fresh ginger, hot mustard.

Makes 4 servings.

VEGETABLES ALI BABA

Preparation Time: 10 minutes
Cooking Time: 18 minutes

4 cups cooked brown rice
  (page 140) or quick rice
2 tablespoons oil
1 medium onion, sliced
2 cloves garlic, sliced
1 carrot, in thin strips
1 small green or red pepper,
  in strips

4 ounces mushrooms, halved
½ cup water chestnuts
1 can (about 3 ounces) quail
  eggs (optional)
1 cup bean sprouts
Soy sauce or tamari

Have brown rice precooked, or cook quick rice. Heat oil in large skillet and stir-fry the onion, garlic, carrot, pepper and mushrooms until crisp-tender, about 6 minutes. Add rice, water chestnuts and quail eggs, toss and reheat. Sprinkle with the sprouts and soy sauce and heat five minutes longer.

Makes 4 servings.

6 *Economical and Quick Meat Favorites*

Meat makes the meal—more than anything else, for many diners. Since meat is so often considered the mainstay of a meal, 42 recipes for meat dishes from Barbecued Meat Buns to Veal Parmigiana are given here.

In many instances, meat is cut thin for fast cooking, and sauced right in the pan. You will find flavors rich and clear—and the nutritional values of the foods, which are often lost in longer cooking, are intact here, for your well-being. A confession: This chapter was finished and practically on its way before I realized that steak was omitted. You'll find the recipes now, but it's a good idea to consider whole, tender steak an occasional choice, rather than your weekly mainstay, if you'd like both a balanced budget and more varied menus.

BARBECUED MEAT BUNS

Preparation Time: 6 minutes
Cooking Time: 7 minutes

¾ pound ready-to-eat ham or other cooked meat
¼ cup red wine or apple-cider vinegar
¼ cup brown sugar
½ cup chili sauce or catsup
1 clove garlic, crushed

1 teaspoon prepared mustard
1 teaspoon Worcestershire sauce
¼ cup strong dark coffee
4 hamburger buns or 8 slices bread, toasted

74

Cut meat into slivers. Combine remaining ingredients, except buns, and bring to a boil. Add meat and heat through. Spoon onto toasted buns or bread.

Makes 4 servings.

BEEF AND BLACK OLIVES

Preparation Time: 10 minutes
Cooking Time: 7 minutes

1 *pound sirloin steak*
¼ *cup butter*
Salt, pepper
⅓ *cup dry red wine*

¼ *cup sliced pitted black olives*
2 *tablespoons chopped parsley*

Slice sirloin into very thin strips across the grain on the diagonal. Brown quickly in hot butter; sprinkle with salt and pepper. Add remaining ingredients and stir over heat to blend.

Makes 4 servings.

BEEF "FILLET"-STYLE ROAST

Preparation Time: 5 minutes
Cooking Time: 16 to 25 minutes

1 *to 1½ pounds beef fillet or strip of sirloin tip or chuck fillet, cut lengthwise in halves*

Pepper
4 *small white onions*

Set oven to preheat to 450° F. Season meat well with freshly ground pepper. Place on rack in pan with small white onions, halved. Pour boiling water under rack in pan. Roast in hot oven, 16 to 25 minutes, until rare-browned. Serve in thin slices.

Makes 4 to 6 servings.

BRACIOLE STEAKS

Preparation Time: 3 minutes
Cooking Time: 5 minutes

1 *pound beef shoulder, sliced
very thin*
Salt, pepper, paprika
4 *tablespoons butter or margarine*

2 *to 3 tablespoons chopped
parsley*

Cut meat into serving portions; season on both sides with salt, pepper and generous amount of paprika. Heat butter in pan until it sizzles, add meat and brown quickly on both sides. Meanwhile, snip parsley with scissors. Remove meat to serving plate, sprinkle with chopped parsley and pour the browned butter over.
Makes 3 to 4 servings.

BURGERS AND VARIATIONS

Preparation Time: 3 minutes
Cooking Time: 10 minutes

1 *pound ground beef*
¼ *cup very cold water*

1 *teaspoon salt*
¼ *teaspoon pepper*

Use ground chuck, sirloin or round. Chuck is fattest and juiciest, sirloin expensive and delicious, round leanest and lowest in calories. Blend lightly with cold water and seasonings. Shape into 4 patties to fit rolls or bread, broil to taste—5 minutes each side for medium rare.

Variations:
Barbecue: Brush with barbecue sauce during broiling.
Cheeseburger: Shape patties around a cube of cheese—anything from Cheddar to Danish blue—before broiling. Or brown second side lightly, top with cheese, finish broiling.

Chinese: Add Chinese vegetables in sauce, top with fried noodles.

Pizza: Top with prepared spaghetti sauce, oregano, good Italian melting cheese—mozzarella, provolone or another. Serve on a toasted English muffin.

Wine: Substitute red wine for the water.

Trimmings: lettuce, watercress, tomato slices, onion rings, stuffed olives, French-fried onion rings, pickle relish, cucumber slices, catsup, mustard, mayonnaise.

CALF'S BRAINS WITH CAPER BUTTER

Preparation Time: 5 minutes
Cooking Time: 25 minutes

1 *pair calf's brains*   2 *tablespoons butter*
Water   1 *tablespoon lemon juice*
Salt   *Capers*
2 *tablespoons vinegar*   *Boiled new potatoes*
¼ *cup seasoned bread crumbs*

Wash brains well (if you have time, soak in acidulated cold water). Cut to separate, and trim large membranes. Place in small pan with cold salted water to cover; add vinegar, bring to boil, simmer 5 minutes. Plunge into cold water to cover. Remove large membranes. Coat brains with seasoned crumbs. (Make these quickly by breaking a slice of bread into the blender container, adding a parsley sprig, basil leaf, or other herbs to taste; blend to crumb.) Heat butter in a small skillet and brown brains on all sides gently, about 8 minutes. Remove to serving plate, turn heat high, add lemon juice to skillet, add capers and a little of their briny juice. Pour sauce over brains. Serve with boiled new potatoes, halved to cook quickly.

Makes 2 servings.

CHILI CON CARNE, TEXAS STYLE

Preparation Time: 8 minutes
Cooking Time: 20 minutes

1 pound ground beef (chuck, round or sirloin)
2 tablespoons oil
1 small green pepper, diced
1 medium onion, diced
1 large clove garlic, crushed

2 tablespoons chili powder
1 teaspoon black pepper
1½ teaspoons salt
1 can (16 ounces) red kidney beans, drained
1 can (16 ounces) tomatoes

Break up beef. Heat oil in deep skillet; brown beef in oil, stirring to cook evenly. Drain off excess fat. Add pepper, onion, garlic, seasonings. Stir to glaze vegetables. Add kidney beans, tomatoes. Cook over moderate heat, stirring often, until blended and thickened in consistency. Serve in bowls with crisp crackers, crushed red pepper.
Makes 4 servings.

FLANK STEAK

Preparation Time: 10 minutes
Cooking Time: 9 minutes

3 tablespoons oil
1 tablespoon vinegar
1 teaspoon salt
⅛ teaspoon pepper
¼ teaspoon rosemary

¼ teaspoon basil
1 clove garlic, mashed
1 flank steak, about 1½ pounds

Blend oil, vinegar and seasonings. Pierce flank steak with fork, then turn in marinade to coat all sides. Let stand a few minutes. Preheat broiler. Broil 3 inches from the heat, about 5 minutes; turn, brush with marinade, and brown other side 4 minutes. Flank steak should be pink in the middle; don't overcook. Cut into very thin diagonal slices.
Makes 6 servings. Leftovers are delicious cold, for sandwiches.

FONDUE BOURGUIGNONNE

Preparation Time: 10 minutes
Cooking Time: At the table

4 ounces lean tender beef or
  lamb from leg per person, cut
  into 1½-inch cubes
Scallions

Salt, black pepper
1 cup oil
½ cup butter
Sauces for dipping

Trim the meat cubes of fat, if necessary. Arrange in a mound on a platter; garnish with sliced scallions. At the table, sprinkle meat lightly with salt and pepper. Heat oil and butter in a deep fondue pot. Skim off foam. Keep pot simmering throughout the meal. Each diner spears a cube of meat with a long wooden pick or dipping fork, then holds it in the hot fat about 1 minute until cooked. As each cube of meat is cooked, slip meat from cooking fork to cool eating fork, dip into sauce. Serve with French bread and a finger salad—radishes, cucumber chunks, carrot curls, cherry tomatoes.

Dipping Sauces:
  Steak Sauce
  Prepared mustard combined with mayonnaise and dill
  Pesto Sauce (page 228)

GREEN PEPPER STEAK

Preparation Time: 10 minutes
Cooking Time: 8 minutes

1 pound round steak, ¼ inch
  thick
4 tablespoons soy sauce
1 tablespoon oil

1 green pepper, cut into strips
1 cup water
1 tablespoon cornstarch

Cut steaks into strips about 2 inches long and 1 inch wide. Toss with soy sauce. Heat oil; brown meat strips on one side. Add green pepper and brown with meat, turning to cook both sides. Stir water with cornstarch, add to pan, stir, and cook until peppers are tender and sauce thickened, about 3 minutes.
Makes 4 servings.

HALF-TIME MEAT LOAF

Preparation Time: 8 minutes
Cooking Time: 20 minutes

1 *pound ground beef*
1 *egg*
1 *slice white bread, crumbled*
¼ *cup milk*
¾ *teaspoon salt*

½ *teaspoon dry mustard*
2 *tablespoons chopped onion*
1 *tablespoon chopped parsley*
¼ *cup catsup*

Blend all ingredients except catsup; shape into 4 small loaves on a greased baking pan. Spoon catsup over loaves. Bake in a moderately hot oven (400° F.) about 20 minutes.
Makes 4 servings.

HAM AND SWEETS

Preparation Time: 8 minutes
Cooking Time: 20 minutes

1 *ready-to-eat ham steak, ½*
   inch thick, about 1¼ pounds
6 *cloves*
1 *tablespoon prepared mustard*

1 *can (1 pound) vacuum-*
   packed sweet potatoes
¼ *cup pancake syrup*
1¼ *cups orange juice*

Preheat oven to 450° F. Arrange ham steak on a greased baking dish that can be brought to the table. Stud fat with cloves, spread meat with mustard. Arrange sweet potatoes around the ham, pour pancake syrup and orange juice over all. Bake for 20 minutes.

Makes 3 to 4 servings.

HAM STEAK WITH PEACHES

Preparation Time: 3 minutes
Cooking Time: 25 minutes

1 *ham steak, about 1½ pounds*
2 *tablespoons butter*
3 *scallions, chopped*
¼ *cup soy or teriyaki sauce*
6 *canned peach halves*

¼ *cup peach syrup*
⅛ *teaspoon powdered cloves*
⅛ *teaspoon ground ginger*
2 *tablespoons sherry*

Sauté ham in butter until browned on both sides. Add scallions and soy or teriyaki sauce. Simmer over low heat 15 minutes. Add remaining ingredients; cook 2 to 3 minutes until heated through. Remove to platter, arranging peaches around ham and spooning sauce over.

Makes 4 to 6 servings.

HAMBURGER CAPERS

Preparation Time: 9 minutes
Cooking Time: 10 minutes

1½ *pounds ground beef*
1 *teaspoon salt*
¼ *teaspoon pepper*
2 *tablespoons rinsed capers*
¼ *cup red wine*
¼ *cup softened butter*

1 *small garlic clove, mashed*
1 *tablespoon chopped parsley*
1 *loaf French bread*
2 *tomatoes, sliced*
1 *small green pepper, slivered*
1 *onion, in thin rings*

Blend beef with salt, pepper, capers, and wine. Mix butter with garlic and parsley and use to spread a split French loaf. Wrap the bread in foil and heat in the oven. Shape the meat into a loaf slightly longer than the bread; broil until brown on both sides, done to taste. Make a giant sandwich, topping the meat with the vegetables. Cut into slantwise sections to serve.

Makes 6 servings.

HASH

Preparation Time: 12 minutes
Cooking Time: 14 minutes

2 cups diced leftover roast beef
2½ cups diced cooked
  potatoes
1 medium onion, diced
1½ teaspoons salt
Dash of pepper

⅔ cup milk
4 tablespoons Worcestershire
  sauce
½ cup chopped parsley
2 tablespoons shortening or
  beef drippings

Combine all ingredients except fat. Heat shortening or drippings in large, heavy skillet; add hash mixture and press down evenly. Cook over medium heat until crisp and brown on bottom. With spatula, fold over in half like an omelet. Reduce heat; cook about 5 minutes more. Hash should then slip out easily onto platter.

Makes 4 servings.

KIDNEYS AND MUSHROOMS

Preparation Time: 4 minutes
Cooking Time: 8 minutes

4 lamb or veal kidneys
¼ cup butter
¼ cup sliced onions
¼ pound fresh mushrooms,
  sliced (or 4-ounce can,
  drained)

¼ cup sherry
Salt, pepper
Chopped parsley

Store kidneys in cold water in the refrigerator until wanted. Slice, remove membranes, any fat, and tubes. Melt butter in skillet, add onions and cook for 2 minutes. Add kidneys and mushrooms and brown lightly—kidneys should not be overcooked. Add sherry and salt and pepper to taste. Simmer for a minute or two. Sprinkle with chopped parsley.

Makes 2 to 4 servings. Lamb kidneys are small; allow 2 per serving in this recipe.

LAMB CHOPS DIANE

Preparation Time: 3 minutes
Cooking Time: 10 minutes

4 lamb chops (shoulder chops for economy; rib for delicate flavor; loin for special tenderness)
2 tablespoons butter

Juice of ½ lemon
¼ teaspoon pepper
1 tablespoon Worcestershire Sauce
¼ cup chopped parsley

Brown chops quickly in 1 tablespoon butter, 4 minutes each side to the medium-rare stage. Add remaining ingredients and heat, spooning sauce over chops to coat.

Makes 2 to 4 servings.

MINUTE STEAKS DIANE

Preparation Time: 3 minutes
Cooking Time: 5 to 8 minutes

Use minute steaks, pan-brown quickly, then proceed as for Lamb Chops Diane.

LAMB SATAY

Preparation Time: 20 minutes
Cooking Time: 5 minutes

1 *pound boneless lamb*
3 *tablespoons soy sauce*
1 *clove garlic*

Juice of ½ lemon
½ *onion, chopped*
½ *teaspoon salt*

Cut lamb into thin 1-inch squares. Combine remaining ingredients and marinate meat for 15 minutes or longer. Preheat cooker. Thread the squares on thin metal or bamboo skewers and brown in the broiler or over a table hibachi about 5 minutes, turning often and brushing with marinade for moistness. Don't overcook.

Makes main course for 4 or cocktail servings for 8.

LAMB SCALOPPINE

Preparation Time: 8 minutes
Cooking Time: 7 minutes

1 *pound thin lamb slices, cut*
  lengthwise from the leg
½ *cup flour*
Salt, pepper, ginger
2 *eggs*
2 *tablespoons water*

½ *cup fine dry bread crumbs*
2 *tablespoons oil*
2 *tablespoons butter*
½ *pound mushrooms, sliced,*
  or 1 jar (3 *ounces*)
1 *cup Marsala or red wine*

Pound lamb slices so they are uniformly thin. Dip into flour seasoned with salt, pepper and ginger, then into egg beaten with water, and then into bread crumbs. Heat butter and oil in skillet and brown scaloppine quickly on both sides—just about 2 minutes. Remove to serving platter. Brown mushrooms in same pan. Add wine and heat. Pour very hot over scaloppine.

Makes 4 servings.

Tip: Buy a lamb leg, cut off slices needed, freeze the rest for a weekend roast.

LAMB OR VEAL PICCATA

Preparation Time: 2 minutes
Cooking Time: 3 minutes

4 *thin slices lamb or veal*	1 *tablespoon butter*
2 *tablespoons oil*	*Lemon juice*
Salt, pepper	*Parsley*

Turn meat slices in oil to coat; season with salt and pepper. Brown quickly in hot, ridged pan or on griddle or under broiler. Top with butter, lemon juice, parsley.

Makes 2 to 4 servings.

LIVER ALLA VENEZIANA

Preparation Time: 6 minutes
Cooking Time: 4 minutes

1 *pound calf's or beef liver*	2 *medium onions, chopped*
3 *tablespoons butter*	*Salt and pepper*
3 *tablespoons olive oil*	*Flour*

Cut liver crosswise into ¼-inch slices, discarding membrane and veins. Heat butter, oil and onions in skillet over medium heat. Add salt and pepper, stir just until onions begin to turn gold. Dust liver lightly with flour (this is not necessary if liver is very fresh, but advisable if, as is more usual, liver has been frozen). Add liver to onions and brown, turning constantly, 3 to 4 minutes. Do not overcook. Serve liver and onions with their sauce, over hot cooked cornmeal (Polenta, page 143).

Makes 4 servings.

LIVER, APPLES AND ONIONS

Preparation Time: 5 minutes
Cooking Time: 15 minutes

1 *pound beef or other liver*
Seasoned flour
4 *tablespoons butter*
2 *onions, sliced*

2 *apples, sliced*
Salt, pepper
½ *teaspoon sugar*

Have liver cut very thin; cut into serving portions. Coat with flour seasoned with salt and pepper, brown in melted butter, 3 to 5 minutes. Pork liver should be thoroughly cooked, but beef liver is best pink in the middle. Remove liver from skillet. Add onions and apples to skillet, season and add sugar. Cook, covered, about 10 minutes, until just tender. Add liver, heat through.

Makes 4 servings.

MEATBALLS BOURGUIGNONNE

Preparation Time: 10 minutes
Cooking Time: 15 minutes

1 *pound ground beef*
3 *tablespoons dry bread crumbs*
2 *tablespoons milk*
1 *egg, lightly beaten*
½ *teaspoon salt*

½ *teaspoon pepper*
2 *tablespoons oil*
1 *medium onion, chopped*
½ *cup beef bouillon*
½ *cup red wine*

Combine beef, crumbs, milk, egg, salt and pepper. Shape into 1-inch balls. Heat oil in skillet, add meatballs and chopped onion. Cook, turning often with spatula until lightly browned. Add bouillon (made with a cube) and wine. Bring to a boil, spooning sauce over meat, and cook until glazed.

Makes 4 servings.

MINUTE STEW

Preparation Time: 4 minutes
Cooking Time: 5 minutes

4 *minute steaks*
¼ *cup flour*
Salt, pepper, paprika
Pinch thyme or marjoram

4 *tablespoons butter or marga-rine*
½ *cup bouillon or tomato juice or wine, or combination*

Stack steaks and cut into 1-inch strips. Season flour, and roll steak pieces in this. Heat butter or margarine in heavy skillet. Add meat and brown quickly, stirring to brown all sides. Add liquid. Stir and cook, spooning sauce over meat to blend. Serve immediately over rice or noodles.

Makes 2 to 4 servings.

PORK CHINOISE

Preparation Time: 8 minutes
Cooking Time: 15 to 20 minutes

1 *pound boneless pork from the loin*
1 *onion, chopped*
1 *clove garlic, chopped*
¼ *cup soy sauce*

¼ *cup honey*
¼ *cup vinegar*
Pinch of ginger
1 *cup broth*

Remove the fillet from a pork loin roast; the rest of the loin can be roasted as usual, or used like spareribs. Slice the boneless meat ¼ inch thick. Combine remaining ingredients in shallow baking pan. Add meat strips and stir to coat thoroughly. Pan-brown or roast in very hot oven (450°F.) until meat is deep amber-brown, 15 to 20 minutes. Serve with rice.

Makes 4 servings.

PORK CHOPS AND SAUERKRAUT

Preparation Time: 5 minutes
Cooking Time: 25 minutes

2 to 4 pork chops
1 onion, diced
1 apple, diced
1 pound sauerkraut, drained

1 bay leaf
Caraway seeds
½ cup white wine or beer

Cut chops in half and brown quickly. Add onion and apple, turning to glaze. Add sauerkraut, seasonings, white wine or beer, cover and simmer 15 minutes to cook through and blend flavors. Mound on platter to serve, with hearty rye bread or noodles or boiled potatoes. This is a flexible dish, to be stretched with frankfurters or sausages for meal or party. Ham slices may be used in place of pork chops.
Makes 2 to 4 servings.

PORK CHOP DINNER

Preparation Time: 5 minutes
Cooking Time: 16 minutes

4 loin pork chops
Salt, pepper, nutmeg
1 onion, diced

1 apple, cut into wedges
¼ cup dry sherry

Trim excess fat from chops, and heat strips of fat in pan to grease. Discard strips of fat, season chops and add. Brown one side, about 8 minutes. Meanwhile, dice onion and cut apple. Turn chops, add onion and apple, cover, cook until browned and tender, about 7 minutes longer. Add sherry and cook to heat through. If desired, heat canned yams in pan with chops.
Makes 4 servings.

SALISBURY STEAK

Preparation Time: 5 minutes
Cooking Time: 10 to 12 minutes

1 *pound lean ground beef*
1 *to 2 tablespoons chopped green onion*
1 *tablespoon chopped green pepper*

2 *teaspoons chopped parsley*
½ *teaspoon salt*
Pinches of paprika, pepper, and powdered thyme

Blend ingredients with a fork, shape into 3 thick oval cakes and brown in hot skillet, on one side. Turn.

SALISBURY SAUCE

1 *tablespoon butter*
3 *tablespoons catsup*
2 *teaspoons lemon juice*
½ *teaspoon prepared mustard*

Salt, pepper
1 *tablespoon* Worcestershire *sauce*

Add butter to skillet, melt, add remaining ingredients, heat through and spoon over steak as it finishes on second side, about 5 minutes longer.

Makes 3 servings.

SHISH KEBAB

Preparation Time: 15 minutes
Cooking Time: 12 minutes

1½ pounds lamb cubes
½ cup wine vinegar
½ cup oil
1 clove garlic, crushed
1 teaspoon salt
¼ teaspoon pepper
½ teaspoon oregano

½ teaspoon paprika
3 onions, quartered
12 tomato wedges or cherry tomatoes
1 green pepper, cut into 6 strips

Have lamb cut into 1½-inch cubes. Combine vinegar, oil, garlic and seasonings in bowl (*shortcut:* use 1 cup prepared French dressing), add meat and toss to coat all sides. Arrange meat on 6 skewers alternately with vegetables. Broil close to heat until meat is browned, but still pink in the middle, about 12 minutes, turning often and brushing with marinade for moistness.
    Makes 6 servings.

SLOPPY JOES

Preparation Time: 6 minutes
Cooking Time: 15 minutes

1 tablespoon oil
1 pound ground chuck
1 medium onion, diced
1 clove garlic, mashed
1 teaspoon salt
½ green pepper, diced

1 teaspoon chili powder
Pinch each of oregano and cloves
Parsley flakes
1 can (16 ounces) tomatoes in puree

Heat oil in skillet. Add meat and break up with a wooden spoon. Cook until meat loses its red color, about 5 minutes, stirring occasionally. Meanwhile, peel and dice onion, peel garlic and mash with salt, using side of knife blade. Dice green pepper. Drain excess fat from meat, add vegetables and seasonings, and stir well to combine. Add tomatoes and puree, bring quickly to a boil, and cook, stirring, until slightly thickened and blended, about 10 minutes. Spoon over toasted buns or cooked rice or cooked cornmeal.

Makes 3 to 4 servings.

Tip: To stretch for 6 servings, add 1 can (1 pound) pork and beans after adding tomatoes.

SPAGHETTI AND MEATBALLS

Preparation Time: 6 minutes
Cooking Time: 12 to 15 minutes

1 *pound ground beef*	¼ *teaspoon pepper*
⅓ *cup soft bread crumbs*	*Parsley flakes*
1 *jar* (16 *ounces*) *spaghetti*	*Oregano*
sauce	1 *onion, chopped*
1 *egg*	1 *clove garlic, mashed*
1 *teaspoon salt*	2 *tablespoons oil*

Blend beef, crumbs, ¼ cup of the sauce, egg, seasonings, onion and garlic, beating with a fork. Shape into 1-inch balls. Heat oil in skillet, brown meatballs on all sides, turning often with a spatula. Drain excess fat. Add remaining sauce to the skillet and heat, spooning sauce over meatballs. Serve with hot boiled spaghetti.

Makes 4 servings.

SPAGHETTI AND MEAT SAUCE

Preparation Time: 3 minutes
Cooking Time: 12 minutes

Using the same ingredients as above, except egg, first brown meat in hot skillet, drain excess fat; add crumbs, seasonings, sauce; cook until well blended, about 10 minutes. Serve over hot cooked spaghetti.

Makes 4 servings.

STEAK

Preparation Time: 2 minutes
Cooking Time: 5 to 12 minutes

Thin cut of beef or lamb, ¼   Salt, pepper
to ¾ inches—anything from
minute steak to rib steak

Steaks may be pan-browned, sautéed or oven-grilled. In addition to sirloin, porterhouse, T-bone steaks, club steaks, less expensive cuts from chuck or shoulder may be grilled—especially if cut thin and quickly browned just to the rare state. For greatest economy, buy a roasting cut and slice crosswise into steaks. Slash fat of thick steaks to prevent curling.

To pan-brown: Preheat skillet covered with thin layer of salt, brown steak, first on one side, then the second, just to degree of desired doneness. Allow 2 to 3 minutes each side for very thin steaks, 5 to 6 minutes each side for thicker cuts.

To sauté: Brown in butter or oil, season after turning.

To grill: Preheat broiler. Brown one side, season, turn, and grill second side. Top with pat of butter, slice thick steaks crosswise to serve.

STEAK AU POIVRE

Preparation Time: 5 minutes
Cooking Time: 12 minutes

2-*pound porterhouse or sirloin*
  steak, or 4 small steaks, cut
  1½ inches thick
4 *teaspoons peppercorns*

Salt
2 *tablespoons butter*
¼ *cup Cognac or Bourbon*

Trim fat edges of steak. Crush peppercorns with a rolling pin or with hammer in paper bag. Press into each side of steak, dividing evenly. Heat a heavy skillet, greasing with fat trimmings. Cook the steak about 5 minutes each side, or to desired degree of doneness. Remove to hot platter and season with salt. Heat butter in skillet, add Cognac or Bourbon, heat, then tilt pan slightly to flame to ignite. Pour, flaming, over steak. When flames die down, cut in even slices across the grain and serve.

Makes 4 servings.

STEAK TARTARE

Preparation Time: 5 minutes
Cooking Time: None

1 *pound lean ground round*
  steak
Salt
Freshly ground pepper
Chopped onion to taste

1 *egg*
3 *anchovies, chopped*
Worcestershire sauce
Lemon wedges
Capers

Season steak with salt, pepper, chopped onion. Mound on board, make an indent in center, and work in egg, chopped anchovies, Worcestershire. Remound. Serve with lemon wedges, capers, thin-sliced black bread.

Makes 3 to 4 servings.

SWEDISH MEATBALLS

Preparation Time: 15 minutes
Cooking Time: 15 minutes

1 *pound meatloaf mixture, or*
  ½ pound ground beef, ¼
  pound ground veal, ¼
  pound ground lean pork
½ *cup milk*
1 *egg*
½ *cup fine dry bread crumbs*
1 *teaspoon prepared mustard*

1 *teaspoon salt*
½ *teaspoon pepper*
⅛ *teaspoon nutmeg*
4 *tablespoons butter*
1 *medium onion, chopped*
1 *tablespoon flour*
½ *cup light cream*

Break up meat with fork. Beat milk with egg and add crumbs (quickest in the blender). Add seasonings to meat. Melt 2 tablespoons butter in a skillet and brown chopped onion lightly. Add to meat, then add crumb mixture. Blend well and shape into small balls, about ½ inch in diameter. Roll lightly in flour. Melt 2 tablespoons butter in the same skillet and brown the meatballs lightly on all sides, turning with a slotted spatula. Add cream and stir smooth; simmer about 5 minutes, spooning sauce over meatballs.

Makes 4 servings.

TONGUE WITH RAISIN SAUCE

Preparation Time: 5 minutes
Cooking Time: 20 minutes

1 *package precooked tongue,*
  about 2 pounds
2½ *cups water*
¼ *cup cider vinegar*

¼ *cup brown sugar*
¼ *cup seedless raisins*
6 *gingersnaps, crumbled*

Place precooked tongue with water in a small pan. Bring to boil, lower heat, and simmer about 8 minutes. Remove tongue to platter. Add remaining ingredients for sauce to pan, heat and stir to blend. Slice tongue, arrange in sauce, heat through.

Makes 4 servings.

VEAL CORDON BLEU

Preparation Time: 10 minutes
Cooking Time: 10 minutes

1 *pound veal scaloppine* (8 *slices*)	2 *eggs*
4 *slices Swiss cheese*	1 *tablespoon water*
4 *slices ham*	½ *cup fine dry bread crumbs*
½ *cup flour seasoned with salt, pepper, nutmeg*	½ *cup butter*

Have veal cut into 8 uniform thin slices; pound to flatten and tenderize. Sandwich cheese and ham between slices of veal and pound the edges together to seal the package. Coat with seasoned flour. Dip into eggs lightly beaten with 1 tablespoon water, then into bread crumbs, coating thickly. Brown slowly in hot butter, about 10 minutes in all.

Makes 4 servings.

VEAL PARMIGIANA

Preparation Time: 6 minutes
Cooking Time: 15 minutes

1 *pound thin-sliced veal scaloppine*	1 *clove garlic*
1 *egg, lightly beaten*	1 *jar* (16 *ounces*) *marinara sauce*
¼ *cup bread crumbs*	¼ *pound mozzarella cheese*
¼ *cup grated Parmesan cheese*	¼ *cup grated Parmesan cheese for topping*
¼ *cup oil*	
1 *small onion*	

Have veal pounded for extra thinness and tenderness. Dip into beaten egg, then into bread crumbs mixed with Parmesan cheese. Heat oil and brown veal on both sides. Remove to a shallow bake-and-serve dish large enough to hold the meat in a single layer. In the skillet, brown onion and garlic lightly, add marinara sauce and simmer 5 minutes. Pour sauce over meat, top with mozzarella and Parmesan and set under broiler uncovered, until the cheese melts, about 5 minutes.

Makes 4 servings.

For Chicken Scaloppine, *see* page 103.

Party Specialties

HAM FOR A BUFFET

Preparation Time: 5 minutes
Cooking Time: 25 minutes

5-pound canned ham
1 cup orange marmalade

¼ cup mustard
1 teaspoon cloves

Remove ham from can. Strip off gelatin on surface. Set in moderately hot oven (375° F.) until glaze melts. Combine marmalade and seasonings, spoon over ham and return to oven to glaze, about 20 minutes. Slice thinly.

Makes about 20 servings.

Tip: Have butcher pre-slice canned ham, tie together in original shape, then prepare as above. Cut string and remove at serving time.

JAMBALAYA FOR 12

Preparation Time: 10 minutes
Cooking Time: 25 minutes

1 *pound hot Italian sausage,*
cut into chunks
2 *large red onions, diced*
1 *green pepper, diced*
4 *tablespoons oil*
2 *cups raw rice*
2 *pounds canned or boiled*
ham, in chunks
3½ *cups hot bouillon*
1 *can (1 pound) tomatoes in*
sauce

¾ *cup dry white wine*
¾ *teaspoon each thyme, basil,*
salt
¼ *teaspoon each pepper,*
cayenne pepper, ground
cloves
1½ *pounds cleaned and*
deveined shrimp

Brown sausage in Dutch oven, drain off excess fat. Stir in onions and pepper. Add oil and rice, heat and stir to glaze. Stir in ham cubes. Add bouillon, tomatoes, wine, seasonings. Cover and cook 15 minutes, until rice is tender. Add shrimp for last 5 minutes of cooking time.

Makes 12 servings.

7 *Poultry Plus*

"Cut it thin and cook it fast" applies to poultry, too. You will find chicken breasts easy to bone; you can do this with your fingers and an occasional assist from a small, sharp-pointed knife or scissors. However, for economy, a cut-up small chicken is generally a better buy and simple to cut apart with scissors or a cleaver. Basic fried chicken, broiled chicken, and flavorful bakes are all feasible in one-half hour.

Today's young birds (and this applies to turkey meat and duckling, as well as chicken) are tender enough to cook in short order, and they take well to simple seasonings from butter to soy sauce. And don't overlook the versatile livers, which cook quickly into satisfying meals—or even a rotisseried chicken from the deli, transformed with your easy saucery.

BAKED BREAST OF CHICKEN IN WINE

Preparation Time: 5 minutes
Cooking Time: 25 minutes

2 chicken breasts	2 tablespoons flour
Salt, pepper, paprika	½ cup chicken bouillon
¼ cup butter	½ cup white wine
2 tablespoons butter for sauce	½ tablespoon chopped parsley

Preheat oven to 400° F. Remove bones from chicken breasts; split breasts in half and then in quarters. Season with salt, pepper and paprika. Arrange chicken on a buttered baking pan, dot with the ¼ cup butter. Bake in hot oven, uncovered, for 15 minutes. Meanwhile, melt the 2 tablespoons butter, stir in flour, and cook for a minute or two. Stir in bouillon (made with cubes), and wine and cook, stirring, until the sauce is thickened and smooth. Add parsley. Pour the sauce over the chicken, cover the pan tightly, and bake 10 minutes longer, until the chicken is cooked through.

Makes 4 servings.

BAKED CHICKEN

Preparation Time: 5 minutes
Cooking Time: 25 minutes

1 *fryer chicken, about 2½* *pounds, cut up*	1 *tablespoon* Worcestershire *sauce*
Salt, pepper	½ *orange*
Butter	½ *lemon*

Set oven to preheat to 425° F. Separate chickens at joints, split breast, and season with salt and pepper. Rub foil-lined baking pan with butter, spread out chicken pieces, sprinkle with Worcestershire sauce, squeeze juice of orange and lemons over. Dot top with butter. Bake in very hot oven, about 22 minutes, until tender.

Makes 4 servings.

BARBECUED CHICKEN WINGS

Preparation Time: 10 minutes
Cooking Time: 20 minutes

2 *pounds chicken wings*	2 *tablespoons lemon juice*
½ *cup soy sauce*	2 *tablespoons sherry*
½ *cup honey*	1 *teaspoon dry mustard*

Marinate chicken wings at room temperature in a sauce made of remaining ingredients for 8 minutes or longer, if possible. Turn and baste to coat well. Arrange on a foil-lined broiler pan and broil 5 inches from the heat, turning and basting often, until crisp and cooked through, about 20 minutes. Serve hot or at room temperature.

Makes 4 to 6 servings.

BROILED CHICKEN OREGANO

Preparation Time: 5 minutes
Cooking Time: 25 minutes

1 *broiler chicken, 2 pounds*
½ *cup oil*
1 *clove garlic, crushed*
1 *teaspoon salt*

2 *teaspoons dried oregano* (*or*
tarragon)
Dash of pepper

Split and quarter a tender young chicken and arrange on an oiled broiler rack, skin side down. Combine the remaining ingredients, in advance if possible, to make a basting sauce. Broil the chicken for about 25 minutes, about 6 inches from the heat, turning and basting it often with the sauce, until it tests done —insert a fork at the leg joint; the juices should run clear, without a trace of pink.

Makes 2 to 4 servings.

Broiled Chicken Variations:

1. Rub skin with lemon juice, spread with butter. Season with salt, pepper, paprika and sugar—2 teaspoons to a chicken. Broil as directed, brushing with pan drippings.

2. Devil the chicken with a basting sauce made of ½ cup oil, 1 teaspoon each salt and paprika, ¼ teaspoon each mustard and Tabasco, 1 tablespoon vinegar.

3. *Broiled Chicken Paprikash:* Make sauce of ½ cup oil, 2 tablespoons lemon juice, 1 tablespoon flour, 1 teaspoon

salt, 2 teaspoons paprika. Brush on chicken before and
during broiling.

CHICKEN CACCIATORE

Preparation Time: 5 minutes
Cooking Time: 25 minutes

1 *chicken, 2½ pounds*
Flour, salt, pepper
4 tablespoons oil

1 *can (4 ounces) mushrooms*
1 *can (8 ounces) tomato*
sauce with peppers

Cut chicken into quarters and remove as many bones as possible.
Cut breasts into 4 pieces, and separate legs and thighs. Coat the
chicken pieces with seasoned flour and brown quickly on all sides
in oil. Add mushrooms with their liquid and tomato sauce. Cover
and simmer 15 minutes.
Makes 4 servings.

CHICKEN CURRY

Preparation Time: 10 minutes
Cooking Time: 20 minutes

1 *broiler chicken, about 2*
pounds, cut up
4 tablespoons oil
2 onions, chopped
2 tart apples, peeled and
chopped

3 tablespoons curry powder
Salt, pepper
Dash of cinnamon
1 *can (4 ounces) sliced mush-*
rooms
2 cups instant broth

Cut chicken from large bones in chunks. Brown quickly in oil in
pan. Add onions, apples, and sauté a minute or two. Stir in
curry powder, other seasonings, and mushrooms. Add broth,
cover and cook about 15 minutes. Serve with rice and raisins,
shredded coconut, chutney.
Makes 3 servings.

CHICKEN LIVERS WITH OLIVES

Preparation Time: 5 minutes
Cooking Time: 10 minutes

4 slices bacon
2 tablespoons chopped onion
2 tablespoons chopped green
  pepper
12 chicken livers, halved

Flour, salt, pepper
⅓ cup red wine
⅓ cup sliced pitted black
  olives

Cut bacon into quarters, cook until crisp, drain on paper towels. Add onion and green pepper to fat in skillet, cook until limp. Dredge chicken livers with seasoned flour and brown quickly. Add wine and olives and simmer, covered, for 2 minutes. Serve on rice, with bacon quarters as a topper.
  Makes 4 servings.

CHICKEN MOO GOO GAI PAN (CHINESE STYLE CHICKEN WITH VEGETABLES)

Preparation Time: 12 minutes
Cooking Time: 10 minutes

2 whole chicken breasts, boned
  and skinned, cut into 2-inch
  squares
½ teaspoon salt
1 teaspoon cornstarch
2 tablespoons oil
1 cup celery, sliced diagonally
1 can (4 ounces) button mushrooms

1 green pepper, cut in squares
1 can (5 ounces) water chestnuts, drained
1 tablespoon soy sauce
1 tablespoon cornstarch
1 cup chicken broth
¼ cup blanched, toasted
  almonds

3 T soy
1 t. ginger

Cut up chicken and shake in a bag with salt and cornstarch. Stir-fry in hot oil until chicken turns white, about 2 minutes. Add celery, cook 2 minutes. Add mushrooms with liquid, green pepper, water chestnuts and soy sauce stirred with cornstarch. Add chicken broth. Cook 4 minutes more. Add almonds.

Makes 4 servings.

CHICKEN OR TURKEY SCALOPPINE

Preparation Time: 5 minutes
Cooking Time: 8 minutes

¾ *pound chicken or turkey breast*	½ *cup seasoned soft bread crumbs*
1 *egg*	3 *tablespoons oil*
Salt, pepper	3 *tablespoons sherry*
1 *tablespoon sour cream*	

Cut raw chicken or turkey in very thin slices, as for scaloppine. Beat egg with salt, pepper and cream. Dip slices in this, then in bread crumbs. Heat oil in skillet and brown scaloppine slices quickly. Add sherry, spooning over chicken, heating until glazed.

Makes 2 servings.

CHICKEN PAPRIKASH—QUICK

Preparation Time: 5 minutes
Cooking Time: 25 minutes

4 *chicken breast halves, boned*	1 *tablespoon sweet paprika*
2 *tablespoons oil*	1 *tablespoon flour*
1 *small onion, sliced*	⅔ *cup chicken bouillon*
1 *carrot, sliced thin*	⅓ *cup sour cream*
¼ *cup sliced celery*	*Salt, pepper*

Split chicken breast pieces. Heat oil in a skillet. Brown the chicken pieces and move to side of pan. Add onion, carrot and celery and cook until onion is transparent. Sprinkle with paprika and flour and stir for a minute. Dissolve a chicken bouillon cube in ⅔ cup hot water; add to skillet and cook, stirring, until sauce is thickened. Spread chicken pieces in pan and spoon sauce over. Cover and simmer for 10 minutes. Add sour cream and salt and pepper to taste. Heat all together without boiling. Serve with rice or noodles.

Makes 4 servings.

CHICKEN TEMPURA

Preparation Time: 12 minutes
Cooking Time: 15 minutes

3 eggs
1 cup water
⅓ teaspoon baking powder
1½ cups flour

⅓ teaspoon salt
2 chicken breasts
Fat for deep frying
Vegetable pieces (see below)

Beat eggs and water with a fork; stir in baking powder, flour, salt lightly—lumps don't matter. Bone chicken breasts, split, then cut each half into 4. Dip pieces into batter and fry in enough deep hot fat (375°F.) to cover the chicken, until the coating is brown and crisp, about 10 minutes.

Use leftover batter to dip eggplant sticks, whole green beans, or thin slices of sweet potato for frying. Keep the chicken hot in a moderately slow oven (325°F.) while you fry the vegetable tempura.

CHICKEN TERIYAKI

Preparation Time: 8 minutes
Cooking Time: 3 minutes

¾-pound boneless breast of
chicken

½ cup bottled Teriyaki Sauce

Cut chicken into thin strips. Toss with sauce in shallow pan. Cook under broiler until tender, about 3 minutes.

Makes 2 servings.

CHINESE CHICKEN

Preparation Time: 12 minutes
Cooking Time: 17 minutes

As in most Chinese cooking, preparation time is comparatively lengthy, cooking time brief. The vegetables should be prepared in advance.

2-pound fryer chicken	*1 green pepper*
2 teaspoons salt	*2 cups celery*
½ teaspoon pepper	*½ cup chicken broth*
2 tablespoons lemon juice	*1 tablespoon cornstarch*
1 teaspoon sugar	*3 tablespoons soy sauce*
3 tablespoons oil	*2 fresh tomatoes*

Cut chicken in small serving pieces, cutting through bones with poultry shears or cleaver. Season with salt, pepper, lemon juice and sugar. Heat oil in deep skillet and brown chicken quickly on all sides. Meanwhile, cut up pepper and celery. Add vegetables and chicken broth, cover the skillet and simmer 10 minutes. Blend cornstarch and soy sauce and stir in; cook, stirring, until sauce is clear. Add tomatoes cut in wedges and cook a minute or two longer. Serve with rice.

Makes 4 servings.

CURRIED CHICKEN SALAD

Preparation Time: 10 minutes
Cooking Time: None

1½ cups cold diced cooked or
  canned chicken
¼ cup celery, diced
1 green onion, sliced thinly
¼ cup green grapes

½ cup mayonnaise
¼ cup sour cream or yogurt
1 teaspoon curry powder
Lettuce

Combine chicken, celery, onion, grapes in bowl. Stir mayonnaise, sour cream and curry powder together. Add to chicken and stir to combine. Serve on lettuce with black olives.
  Makes 2 servings.

DEVILED CHICKEN BREASTS

Preparation Time: 6 minutes
Cooking Time: 20 minutes

2 chicken breasts
Salt, pepper

Prepared mustard
1 cup dry bread crumbs

Remove bones from chicken breasts, split in half, and cut each half into 2 pieces. Sprinkle with salt and pepper, and coat thinly with prepared mustard. Dip into bread crumbs, firmly. Fry in hot fat, 1 inch deep, until brown and crisp, about 20 minutes.
  Makes 4 servings.

FRIED CHICKEN

Preparation Time: 5 minutes
Cooking Time: 25 minutes

½ cup flour
¼ teaspoon pepper
1½ teaspoons salt

1 chicken, 2½ pounds, quartered

Combine flour and seasonings in paper bag. Cut apart chicken breast sections at wing joints, making four pieces; separate thighs and legs. Shake, a few pieces at a time, in bag with seasoned flour. Heat fat to depth of 1½ inches in pan, drop chicken pieces in and cook over medium-hot heat, turning to brown all sides, about 25 minutes. Serve piping hot.

Makes 4 servings.

GRILLED DUCKLING

Preparation Time: 5 minutes
Cooking Time: 25 minutes

1 *duckling, about 4 pounds,*
   quartered
Salt, pepper
Soy sauce

½ *can frozen orange juice con-*
   centrate
½ *cup honey*

Separate duckling quarters at all joints. Sprinkle with salt and pepper, rub with soy sauce, arrange on a rack on a foil-lined broiling pan, 5 inches from the heat. Broil, turning occasionally, until browned and tender, about 20 minutes. Spoon off fat drippings and reserve for another use. Brush with orange juice concentrate and honey, mixed, and broil 5 minutes longer to glaze.

Makes 4 servings.

ROCK CORNISH GAME HENS

Preparation Time: 5 minutes
Cooking Time: 20 to 25 minutes

BROILED

Split birds in half or in quarters, remove as many bones as possible, brush with melted butter, season with salt and pepper. Broil at 6 inches from heat, skin side down, until brown; turn, brush with butter, broil skin side up until crisp-skinned and tender. Allow ½ to 1 bird to a serving.

FRIED

Split hens in half or cut them into quarters; fry as you would chicken.

TURKEY STEAK BARBECUE

Preparation Time: 3 minutes
Cooking Time: 25 minutes

1 *frozen turkey steak*
½ *cup oil-and-vinegar dressing*
  or barbecue sauce

¼ *cup butter, melted*
  (*optional*)
¼ *cup white wine* (*optional*)

Have the meat man cut the breast half of a frozen turkey into inch-thick crosswise steaks. Cut 1 steak in half for a quick barbecue, outdoors or in the oven broiler. Reserve the remainder in the freezer. Brush the steak with vinegar-and-oil dressing, or with your favorite barbecue sauce. Broil 5 inches from the heat, about 20 to 25 minutes, turning and basting often with the marinade or with melted butter mixed with white wine, until the steak is thoroughly cooked and tender.

Makes 2 servings.

8 *Fish Is Quick*

Fish is naturally quick to cook. In fact, fish needn't be cooked at all, if you choose to serve it in Japanese sashimi style—thinly sliced and with a sharp mustard sauce and soy sauce for dipping —or to marinate it ahead.

Whether you choose to pan-brown, sauté in a little butter with a dash of white wine, steam or bake, fish can be done to your taste, and in many flavors, in short order. The half-hour cook will avoid the greatest pitfall of fish cookery—overcooking. Fish that has been cooked quickly retains its moisture and firm texture. In fact, fish is one of the most succulent of all foods.

BAKED FISH FILLETS WITH STUFFING

Preparation Time: 5 minutes
Cooking Time: 16 minutes

½ *package prepared stuffing*
   mix
1 *cup hot water*
4 *fillets of sole, flounder or*
   other lean fish

1 *lemon (juice)*
Salt, paprika
Butter or margarine

Set oven to preheat to 375°F. Grease a shallow baking pan, about 9 x 5 inches. Empty ½ package stuffing mix into pan, add

109

hot water, stir to combine and spread out in pan. Arrange fish fillets on the bed of stuffing. Sprinkle them with the lemon juice, add salt, paprika, dot with butter or margarine. Bake in hot oven for 12 minutes, then brown under the broiler 3 to 4 minutes.

Makes 4 servings.

BAKED RED SNAPPER

Preparation Time: 3 minutes
Cooking Time: 20 minutes

Lay a 3-pound cleaned red snapper or other fish on an oiled baking dish. Season with salt and pepper and dot generously with butter. Pour 1 tablespoon soy sauce and ¼ cup sherry over fish. Bake in a moderately hot oven (400°F.) basting often with the pan juices, about 20 minutes, until golden. Serve with lemon wedges.

Makes 3 to 4 servings.

PETITE BOUILLABAISSE

Preparation Time: 6 minutes
Cooking Time: 20 minutes

4 tablespoons butter
2 medium onions, diced
1 clove garlic, mashed
2 cups water
1 can (1 pound) stewed tomatoes
1 tablespoon salt

¼ teaspoon each pepper, thyme, paprika
2 tablespoons chopped parsley
4 pounds fish, whole assorted varieties, or fillets
French bread

Melt butter in a large pot, glaze onion and garlic in the butter but do not brown; add all ingredients except fish and bread. Bring to a boil and simmer for 10 minutes. Meanwhile, cut fish into sections, add, and cook about 10 minutes longer, until the fish is cooked through and flakes readily at the touch of a fork. Serve in soup plates, with toasted French bread for dunking.

Makes 6 servings.

Note: The fish for a true *grande bouillabaisse* is always cut into chunks, bones and all, and includes clams, shrimp and lobster, as available, plus a pinch of saffron.

BROILED FISH STEAKS

Preparation Time: 2 minutes
Cooking Time: 10 to 12 minutes

Sprinkle ¾-inch-thick fish steaks (salmon, halibut or cod) with lemon juice, brush with butter or oil, season with salt and pepper. Broil about 5 minutes on each side, turning once. When done, fish should be opaque and lightly browned. Top with a pat of butter, sprinkle with parsley. Serve with lemon wedges.

Allow 6 ounces fish steak per serving.

CLAM FRITTERS

Preparation Time: 5 minutes
Cooking Time: 6 minutes

1 can (8 ounces) chopped
   clams
2 eggs, beaten
½ teaspoon salt

Pepper
1¼ cups flour
1½ teaspoon double-acting
   baking powder

Combine the clams and their broth with eggs, salt and pepper. Mix flour and baking powder and blend with clam mixture to make a light batter. Drop by spoonfuls into deep hot fat (375°F.) and fry until golden.

Makes 4 servings.

CLAMS POSILIPPO

Preparation Time: 10 minutes
Cooking Time: 8 minutes

1 *quart steamer clams*   *Parsley*
1-*pint jar marinara sauce*

Scrub clams and rinse thoroughly until water runs clear. Place in pan that has a tight lid, pour sauce over. Sprinkle with parsley. Cover, bring to boil, cook about 5 minutes, until clams open.
  Makes 2 servings.

CLAMS—STEAMED

Preparation Time: 10 minutes
Cooking Time: 6 minutes

1 *quart steamer clams*   *Dash red-pepper sauce*
2 *cups water*   *Melted butter*
1 *teaspoon salt*

Scrub and rinse clams as above. Add water, salt, red-pepper sauce. Cover, bring to boil. Steam 5 minutes until clams open. Serve with melted butter for dipping clams.
  Makes 2 servings.

CRAB MEAT CASANOVA

Preparation Time: 5 minutes
Cooking Time: 8 minutes

6 *tablespoons butter*   *Crushed red pepper*
1 *onion or 3 scallions, finely*   2 *tablespoons minced parsley*
  chopped   ½ *cup white wine*
1 *pound crab-meat chunks,*   ¼ *cup mayonnaise or sour*
  fresh or frozen   *cream or brandy*
Salt, pepper

Melt butter, sauté chopped onion until golden; add crab meat, toss over heat for 2 minutes. Add salt, red pepper and parsley, and toss. Add white wine; heat, stir. Add mayonnaise or sour cream, stir again and heat through. Or warm brandy in ladle or metal measuring cup, ignite, and pour over crab meat. Stir until flames die down. Serve immediately with toast.

Makes 4 servings.

DEVILED CRAB PUFF

Preparation Time: 7 minutes
Cooking Time: 10 minutes

1 *pound cooked frozen crab* *meat*	1 *teaspoon prepared mustard* *Salt, pepper, Tabasco to taste*
2 *eggs*	2 *tablespoons butter*
½ *cup cream (or half-and-half)*	1 *cup soft fine bread crumbs*
1 *tablespoon minced onion*	

Preheat oven to 350°F. Pick over crab meat to remove bits of shells and membranes. Beat eggs with cream and seasonings and combine with crab meat. Divide mixture into 6 individual shells or baking dishes. Melt butter and toss with bread crumbs; top shells thickly. Bake in a moderate oven (350°F.) until the crumb topping is crisply browned and the crab piping hot, about 10 minutes.

Makes 6 servings.

Shortcut: Combine crab meat with ¾ cup mayonnaise in place of eggs and cream. Omit salt and pepper. Prepare as above.

FISH AND CHIPS

Preparation Time: 4 minutes
Cooking Time: 5 minutes

1 *pound fillet of flounder, or other white fish*	¾ *cup dry crumbs or pancake mix*
1 *egg*	1 *teaspoon salt*
1 *tablespoon lemon juice*	1/16 *teaspoon grated nutmeg*
	Pepper

Wipe the fish dry. Beat egg and lemon juice and combine crumbs or pancake mix with seasonings. Dip fish into crumbs, then into egg, and again in crumbs, pressing firmly. Shake excess crumbs off. Fry in deep hot fat to cover (375°F.) until brown and crisp, about 5 minutes. Drain on paper towels. Serve with French fried potatoes (the chips) and vinegar or Tartar Sauce, below.

TARTAR SAUCE

Blend ¾ cup mayonnaise with 1 teaspoon each finely chopped green pepper, green olives and pickles. Serve with fish above, or any simple fish preparation.

SMELT FRY

Preparation Time: 4 minutes
Cooking Time: 5 minutes

Wash and dry the fish, then proceed as for Fish and Chips.

FISH FILLETS MARGUERY

Preparation Time: 6 minutes
Cooking Time: 24 minutes

1 pound sole or flounder fillet
2 tablespoons flour
Salt, pepper
4 tablespoons butter
4 green onions, sliced

1½ cups mushrooms, sliced
1 pound raw shrimp shelled
and deveined
1 cup heavy cream
¼ cup white wine

Cut the fish fillets in half lengthwise, coat with flour seasoned with salt and pepper, and brown quickly in a skillet in 2 tablespoons melted butter. Remove to a 1½-quart casserole. Set oven to 425°F. to preheat. Melt a second tablespoon of butter in the same skillet and sauté the onions and mushrooms until lightly browned. Spoon over fish in pan. Add remaining tablespoon butter to the skillet and cook the shrimp just until they turn pink. Add them to the baking dish. Add cream and wine to skillet, heat, stirring, but do not boil. Pour over the contents of pan. Bake in a hot oven for 15 minutes.

Makes 6 servings.

FISH FILLETS BONNE FEMME

Preparation Time: 7 minutes
Cooking Time: 17 minutes

1 pound fish fillets
Salt, pepper
1 cup sliced mushrooms
2 tablespoons minced onion

½ cup white wine
2 teaspoons lemon juice
1 tablespoon butter
1 teaspoon flour

Season the fish fillets with salt and pepper and lay them side by side in a generously buttered skillet. Add mushrooms, onion, wine, and lemon juice. Cover lightly and cook gently for about 10 minutes, until fish is opaque and flakes at the touch of a fork.

Remove fish to heatproof serving dish. Blend butter and flour with fingers, add this to the pan juices, and cook, stirring, until the sauce is smooth and thickened. Pour the sauce over the fish and brown lightly under the broiler.

Makes 4 servings.

FISH FILLETS SESAME

Preparation Time: 8 minutes
Cooking Time: 7 minutes

1 *pound fish fillets, any kind*
4 *scallions*
3 *small zucchini*
½ *red pepper, in strips*
2 *tablespoons oil*

¼ *cup soy sauce*
¼ *cup sherry*
2 *tablespoons toasted sesame seeds*

Cut fish into thin strips. Clean and cut up scallions. Cut zucchini and pepper in long strips. Heat oil in skillet, add vegetables and stir-fry about 2 minutes. Add fish strips and turn to cook all sides, about 3 minutes. Add soy sauce and sherry, heat through. Sprinkle toasted sesame seeds over. Serve with rice.

Makes 4 servings.

FISH FILLETS VERONIQUE

Preparation Time: 3 minutes
Cooking Time: 8 minutes

2 *tablespoons butter*
Fillet of sole or flounder
Flour, salt, pepper

Butter
⅓ *cup seedless white grapes*
1 *tablespoon vermouth*

Heat butter in skillet. For each serving, dust a fillet with seasoned flour and sauté in butter. Remove to a hot dish and melt a little fresh butter in the pan. Add grapes. Cook for 2 minutes, add vermouth and heat. Pour over the fillet.

Makes 1 serving.

FISH IN FOIL

Preparation Time: 4 minutes
Cooking Time: 20 minutes

4 fish steaks (salmon, halibut, cod) ¾ inch thick
¼ cup white wine
¼ cup oil

⅛ teaspoon each rosemary and pepper
4 thin slices lemon

Place each steak on square of oiled aluminum foil. Combine wine, oil and seasonings, pour over steaks. Top with lemon slices. Fold foil to seal package. Bake at 425°F., 15 to 20 minutes, until fish flakes easily.

Makes 4 servings.

FISH FILLETS IN FOIL WITH MUSHROOMS

Make Fish in Foil, above, with fish fillets, 6 ounces per serving, adding to each packet 2 sliced mushrooms, raw or canned, and slivered scallion. Bake as directed.

MUSSELS IN WHITE WINE

Preparation Time: 15 minutes
Cooking Time: 8 minutes

2 quarts mussels
¼ cup oil
6 cloves garlic

Bunch parsley, snipped
2 cups white wine

Scrub mussels thoroughly, removing beards (this takes longer than the cooking). Rinse, lifting out of water 3 times or more, until water runs clear. Place oil in deep pan that has a tight lid, add minced garlic, mussels, parsley snipped into bits with scissors. Pour wine over. Bring to boil and simmer 5 minutes, until mussels open.

Makes 3 servings.

POACHED FISH WITH CUCUMBER SAUCE

Preparation Time: 5 minutes
Cooking Time: 25 minutes

3 *pounds fresh salmon or bass,*	1 *teaspoon salt*
or large whitings, or red snap-	1 *rib celery with green*
per or salmon steaks, cleaned	1 *carrot*
and washed	1 *onion or leek*
3 *cups water*	1 *cup white wine*
4 *peppercorns*	1 *tablespoon soy sauce*
2 *lemon slices*	

Tie fish in cheesecloth or place on a sturdy plate or rack. Combine water, spices and vegetables in a large skillet or fish poacher. Bring to boil quickly. Add fish in cloth or on plate, pour wine over, then soy sauce. Cover. Simmer 18 minutes, basting occasionally.

While fish cooks, prepare Hollandaise Sauce, Easy Way (page 134). Serve with fish.

Makes 3 to 4 servings.

Tip: Reserve cooking liquid and combine with leftover fish and cream sauce for a soup, or freeze to cook fish another time.

ROCK LOBSTER TAILS

Preparation Time: 5 minutes
Cooking Time: 12 minutes (about)

BOILED

Drop frozen tails into boiling salted water; cook 1 to 1½ minutes for each ounce of weight of the largest tail. Slit tops of shells with scissors and open. Serve with melted butter.

Allow about 6 ounces per serving.

BROILED

Split shells of frozen tails. Arrange shell side down, 3 to 4 inches from heat, and broil for 7 minutes. Turn, brush with butter and broil 5 minutes longer. Season and serve with melted butter.

Allow about 6 ounces per serving.

LOBSTER VERDE

Preparation Time: 15 minutes
Cooking Time: 10 minutes

2 *pounds rock lobster tails,*	2 *tablespoons chopped chives*
shelled and sliced	½ *cup chopped parsley*
2 *cloves garlic, mashed*	1 *lemon, juice and grated rind*
1 *tablespoon vinegar*	¾ *teaspoon salt*
½ *cup oil*	*Pepper*

Cover lobster slices with a marinade made by blending the remaining ingredients. Toss to coat thoroughly; broil 8 to 10 minutes, turning and basting with the marinade.

Makes 6 servings.

SALMON COTE

Preparation Time: 16 minutes
Cooking Time: None

1 pound fresh salmon	2 green onions
2 tablespoons fresh lime juice	Shredded Chinese cabbage or
1 teaspoon coarse salt	lettuce
1 teaspoon sugar	Fresh ground pepper

Skin and bone salmon. Cut in thin diagonal slices, against the grain. Arrange on plate. Make sauce by combining lime juice, coarse salt, sugar, and stirring until blended and slightly thickened. Spoon over slices. Serve with chopped green onions, including tops; garnish with shredded Chinese cabbage or lettuce, pass a pepper mill.
  Makes 2 to 3 main-course servings, 6 appetizers.

SALMON PATTIES

Preparation Time: 5 minutes
Cooking Time: 6 minutes

1-pound can salmon	1 tablespoon chopped onion
½ teaspoon salt	1 well-beaten egg
Cayenne pepper	1 tablespoon chopped parsley
¼ cup crumbled crackers or	Bread crumbs
bread	

Remove skin and bones of salmon. Flake fish, add seasonings, crumbled crackers or bread, onion, egg and parsley, and mix well. Shape into patties. Dip lightly into dry bread crumbs and sauté in hot butter or oil in skillet until golden brown. Serve with lemon wedges or Hollandaise Sauce, Easy Way (page 134).
  Makes 4 servings.

SCAMPI

Preparation Time: 12 to 15 minutes
Cooking Time: 5 minutes

1 pound large shrimp
¼ cup oil
¼ cup white wine

Pinch of oregano leaves
1 clove garlic

Shell and devein raw shrimp, leaving tail on. Arrange side by side in shallow heatproof pan. Blend remaining ingredients, pour over shrimp. Broil 5 inches from the heat until shrimp are pink, about 5 minutes. Serve with cooked rice.

Makes 2 servings.

SHRIMP MARINARA

Preparation Time: 6 minutes
Cooking Time: 10 minutes

3 tablespoons oil
1 garlic clove, minced
1 onion, sliced
¼ green pepper, diced
1 pound raw shrimp, shelled
  and deveined and salted

8 ounces prepared marinara
  sauce
Cooked spaghetti

Heat oil and cook garlic, onion and green pepper until tender. Rinse and add shrimp. Cook, stirring for 2 or 3 minutes, just until the shrimp turn pink. Add sauce, heat through, and serve on cooked spaghetti.

Makes 3 to 4 servings.

Also see Shrimp Marinara with Pasta Shells (page 70).

EGGPLANT AND SHRIMP MARINARA

Preparation Time: 13 minutes
Cooking Time: 16 minutes

For economical party dish, double all ingredients in Shrimp Marinara recipe except shrimp. Cut 1 pound eggplant in strips, season with salt and pepper, brown with onion, garlic and green pepper. Prepare remaining recipe as above.
Makes 8 servings.

SHRIMP OR FISH CREOLE

Preparation Time: 9 minutes
Cooking Time: 18 minutes

2 tablespoons oil
1 onion, chopped
1 clove garlic, minced
1 green pepper, chopped
½ cup slivered celery
1 can (8 ounces) tomato sauce

¾ cup water
1 pound raw shrimp, shelled
    and deveined, or 1 pound
    fish fillets, cut into ½-inch
    strips, or 2 7-ounce cans of
    tuna

Heat oil and cook vegetables slowly until limp and clear. Add tomato sauce and water, bring to a boil, simmer 10 minutes. Add shrimp or fish (fresh or canned). Raw shrimp cooks in less than 5 minutes. Serve on hot rice.
Makes 4 to 6 servings.

SHRIMP SAUTE WITH WHITE WINE

Preparation Time: 3 minutes
Cooking Time: 7 minutes

2 pounds large shrimp, peeled
    and deveined
¼ cup butter
2 cloves garlic, minced

1 cup dry white wine
1 teaspoon salt
¼ teaspoon pepper
1 teaspoon dried basil

Cook shrimp in melted butter with garlic until pink, about 3 minutes. Turn often. Add remaining ingredients, cover, cook about 2 minutes until sauce is hot and shrimp just cooked through. Serve over rice.

Makes 6 servings.

SKEWERED SCALLOPS

Preparation Time: 16 minutes
Cooking Time: 10 minutes

1½ pounds scallops
½ cup oil
¼ cup white wine
Salt, pepper
½ teaspoon chopped dill (dried dill weed)

Green pepper chunks
Onion wedges
Tomato wedges

Wash and drain scallops. Combine oil, wine, salt, pepper and dill, and marinate scallops, green pepper chunks and onion wedges for 10 minutes or longer. Preheat broiler. Thread scallops on skewers with green pepper, onion and tomato wedges, alternating ingredients, and broil about 5 inches from the heat, turning and basting often with the marinade, until the scallops are cooked through, about 8 minutes. Serve with Risotto (page 144).

Makes 6 servings.

STIR-FRIED SHRIMP OR FISH WITH SNOW PEAS

Preparation Time: 5 minutes
Cooking Time: 9 minutes

1 *pound shrimp, shelled and deveined, or 1 pound fish fillets, cut into ½-inch strips*
1 *tablespoon cornstarch*
½ *teaspoon salt*
2 *tablespoons oil*

1 *package frozen snow peas, partially thawed*
2 *tablespoons water*
Salt, pepper
Soy sauce

Toss shrimp or fish strips with cornstarch and salt. Heat oil in skillet, cook shrimp or fish about 2 minutes, stirring constantly, until they turn pink. Remove shrimp or fish. In the same oil, cook snow peas for about 5 minutes, stirring often and adding water as needed to keep the peas moist. When peas are tender, return shrimp or fish to pan, add 2 tablespoons soy sauce, heat together for another minute or two.

Makes 3 to 4 servings.

Scallion or green pepper variation: Dice 1 bunch scallions into 1½-inch diagonal pieces, or cut 1 green pepper into strips; use in place of snow peas in recipe above.

SWORDFISH STEAK* IN TOMATO SAUCE

Preparation Time: 6 minutes
Cooking Time: 20 minutes

2 *swordfish steaks*
Flour, salt, pepper
¼ *cup oil*

2 *medium onions, chopped*
1 *can (8 ounces) tomato sauce*

Dust swordfish steaks lightly with flour seasoned with salt and pepper. Heat oil in large skillet and brown steaks and onions gently. Add tomato sauce and simmer for about 12 minutes, until fish is cooked through.

Makes 2 servings.

*Swordfish is available fresh only in coastal areas.

TROUT SAUTE MEUNIERE

Preparation Time: 3 minutes
Cooking Time: 10 to 12 minutes

Dip cleaned fresh or frozen brook trout, with or without the heads, in flour; shake off excess flour. Then dip into cornmeal seasoned with salt and pepper. Allow 1 fish to a serving. Brown on both sides in half oil, half butter, in a skillet. Remove to a serving dish. Sprinkle with lemon juice and garnish with lemon slices. Heat the butter-oil mixture until well browned, and pour over (this is a lean meal and can use the calories). Sprinkle with chopped parsley.

FISH FILLETS SAUTE MEUNIERE

Follow the recipe above, allowing ¼- to ½-pound fish fillets for each serving.

TROUT SAUTE AMANDINE

Preparation Time: 4 minutes
Cooking Time: 12 minutes

Cook whole trout or fish fillets as for Trout Sauté Meunière. Drain off cooking oil-butter mixture and add 1 tablespoon butter and ½ tablespoon slivered blanched almonds to the pan for each serving. Cook until the almonds are browned. Pour the sauce over the fish and serve.

TUNA-CHEESE BURGERS

Preparation Time: 8 minutes
Cooking Time: 10 minutes

½ cup milk
3 slices bread, with crusts removed
1 small onion, chopped
1 tablespoon chopped parsley

1 tablespoon lemon juice
2 cans (6½ or 7 ounces each) tuna in vegetable oil
6 hamburger buns
6 thin slices sharp American cheese

Pour milk over bread slices in mixing bowl; stir with fork. Add chopped onion. Add parsley flakes, lemon juice. Add tuna; mix well. Spoon mixture onto six bun halves. Place under broiler, heat 6 minutes, or until browned. Top each with cheese slice, broil 4 minutes, until cheese puffs and browns. Brown remaining bun halves at same time. Make sandwiches.

Makes 6 burgers.

TUNA SCALLOP

Preparation Time: 5 minutes
Cooking Time: 18 minutes

1 package (12 ounces) wide egg noodles
¼ pound (½ cup) butter
1 cup grated Cheddar cheese

¼ cup grated Parmesan cheese
2 cans (6 or 7 ounces each) tuna fish
½ cup stuffed green olives

Cook noodles until just tender, drain. Melt butter in saucepan, add noodles, toss. Add cheeses and tuna, toss, shake pan over low heat until all ingredients are warmed through. Pile on hot serving platter, garnish with olives.

Makes 6 servings.

9 *Quick Egg and Cheese Meals*

When it comes to convenience foods, you'd have to look hard to find something better than the quick-cooling egg and/or ready-to-serve or heat-and-eat cheese. Both are complete proteins, handy alternates for meat.

The egg can be served in any state, from barely cooked to hard-cooked, and is the perfect illustration that protein coagulates when heated and toughens with high heat.

Cheese also requires gentle heating, lest it string or curdle.

Herewith, a restrained double dozen of recipes, for any meal from breakfast to midnight supper—restrained because there could be a gross of quick egg and cheese dishes.

If you are worried about cholesterol, bear in mind that low-fat cottage cheese and low-fat mozzarella are largely made with skimmed milk. Eggs have a fair balance of unsaturated as well as saturated fats. If this is really a concern, cook eggs in vegetable oil, rather than butter. Everybody likes a good egg!

Basic Eggs

EGGS COOKED IN THE SHELL—SOFT, MEDIUM OR HARD-COOKED

You may call these "boiled" eggs, but cook them at a simmer—gentle heat produces a more tender cooked egg. Use whole eggs, free of cracks. However you cook them, add cold water to cover eggs, bring quickly to boil, quickly reduce heat to simmer, 3 to 5 minutes for soft-cooked (the longer time for doing a number of eggs in one pan). For medium (white set but yolk still soft) simmer just 6 minutes. For hard-cooked eggs, allow 21 minutes from start in cold water to finish. To shorten time, add eggs to boiling water and simmer just 12 minutes. In any case, plunge eggs promptly into cold water after they are done; crack shells under water for easy peeling.

Bonus: if you cook eggs quickly and gently, and cool them promptly, yolks will be bright yellow and clear—no green ring.

POACHED EGGS

Pour water into skillet to depth of 1 inch and bring to boil, adding 1 tablespoon vinegar per quart. Or use half water and half milk, omitting the vinegar. Stir water with a wooden spoon to create a vortex; drop egg gently into center of swirl. If egg white disperses, fold it in toward center with a spoon, or rotate pan. For extra flavor, add a sprig of any herb you like to the water. Season eggs in pan with salt and pepper. Cook 3 to 5 minutes to desired doneness. For "veiled" egg, spoon water over as egg cooks, or cover pan toward end of cooking. Poached eggs are the base for Eggs Benedict (page 133).

FRIED EGGS

Heat butter or oil in skillet, reduce heat and break eggs into pan. Season with salt and pepper. For "basted" eggs, spoon butter over, cover pan toward end of cooking. For fewer calories, add just enough fat to cover bottom of pan, add eggs, then 2 or 3 tablespoons water, cover pan tightly and steam until eggs are done.

SCRAMBLED EGGS

Beat eggs with 2 tablespoons water or milk per egg; add salt, pepper. Heat butter or oil in skillet, pour beaten eggs in and use a fork or spatula to stir eggs in from sides as they set. Cook just until set to desired doneness.

BAKED EGGS

Break each egg into a greased shallow ramekin or custard cup. Sprinkle with salt and pepper; add tablespoon of tomato sauce or cut-up bacon or cheese. Bake at 325°F. about 12 minutes, or until eggs are set.

CHEESE PUFF

Preparation Time: 7 minutes
Cooking Time: 20 minutes

4 *slices white bread*	3 *eggs*
Butter	½ *teaspoon salt*
1 *small onion, diced*	⅛ *teaspoon pepper*
4 *slices Cheddar or American*	½ *teaspoon paprika*
cheese	1½ *cups milk*

Set oven to preheat to 400° F. Stack bread slices and trim crusts; cut each slice in half. Butter an 8-inch-square pan and spread bread slices in pan. Sprinkle with onion, place cheese slices over. Beat eggs with seasonings and milk, pour over cheese and bread. Bake near bottom of hot oven about 20 minutes, until puffed and golden.

Makes 4 servings.

Note: Flaked cooked or canned fish, crab meat or ham added to the above with onion make a hearty dish.

CHEESE SOUFFLE

Preparation Time: 18 minutes
Cooking Time: 12 minutes

¼ cup butter
¼ cup flour
½ teaspoon chopped fresh
   basil or ¼ teaspoon crumbled dried leaves
½ teaspoon salt
½ teaspoon mustard

½ teaspoon paprika
1 cup milk
1 cup sharp cheese, grated
4 egg yolks
5 egg whites
Dash of salt

Preheat oven to 425° F. Separate eggs; place bowl of egg whites in warm spot. In 2-quart pan heat butter, add flour and stir smooth. Stir in seasonings. Add milk, bring to boil, stirring until smooth and thickened, about 3 minutes. Remove from heat. Stir in cheese briskly. Beat in egg yolks quickly. Beat egg whites with salt until they are stiff but not dry. Fold ¼ of whites into yolk mixture thoroughly, then fold remaining whites in very lightly. Pour into individual soufflé dishes, each holding 1½ cups, filling ¾ full. Bake in hot oven, about 15 minutes, until puffed and golden. Serve immediately. The centers will be slightly runny, the soufflé very lightly puffed, in the French manner.
   Makes 3 servings.

FISH SOUFFLE

Substitute 1 cup cooked or canned fish, flaked, for cheese.

CHICKEN OR MEAT SOUFFLE

Substitute 1 cup cooked or canned chicken or meat, diced, for cheese.

CHEESE STEAKS

Preparation Time: 2 minutes
Cooking Time: 3 minutes

Another great 5-minute meal!

4 *ounces Bel Paese cheese*
1 *egg*
Pepper

Bread or cracker crumbs
Oil or butter for frying

Remove rind, cut cheese into rectangular slices 4 inches long, 2 inches wide, 1 inch thick. Beat egg; season slightly with pepper (no salt is needed). Dip cheese slices in beaten egg, then roll in bread or cracker crumbs. Repeat operation a second time, to coat thoroughly. Fry in ½ inch oil or butter, at high temperature, until golden. Serve immediately.

Makes 1 main-dish serving, 2 snack servings.

CREPES OR BLINTZ WRAPPERS

Preparation Time: 5 minutes to assemble and mix crêpes
Cooking Time: 20 minutes

1 *cup milk or ½ cup milk and*
   ½ cup cream
1 *cup flour*

½ teaspoon salt
2 *eggs plus 3 yolks or 4 eggs*
1 *tablespoon melted butter*

Beat batter ingredients with rotary beater or in blender, just until combined. Use part cream, more egg yolks for richer crêpe batter. Heat 6-inch skillet, melt butter, pour excess into cup, spoon about 2 tablespoons batter into pan, tilt to cover bottom, cook over high heat, raising pan if necessary to prevent scorching, and rotating pan to cook evenly. For crêpes, as soon as top sets, flip to brown other side. For blintzes, brown only one side, turning out onto brown paper as soon as set. Repeat to make about 16. Fold in quarters and heat in Fruit Sauce (page 225) or serve topped with preserves or filled with sweetened ricotta cheese.

BLINTZES

Preparation Time: 15 minutes
Cooking Time: 10 minutes

1 recipe Crêpes or Blintz Wrappers (page 131)

2 *egg yolks or* 1 *egg*	1 *tablespoon cream*
1 *pound cottage cheese*	½ *teaspoon salt*
½ *teaspoon grated lemon rind*	2 *tablespoons sugar*
(*or cut up for blender*)	*Cinnamon*

Beat all ingredients together or combine in blender container; blend about 30 seconds, until smooth. Place a rounded spoonful of filling on cooked side of each pancake. Fold sides over the filling and roll up. Brown quickly in butter. Serve hot, with sour cream and preserves.
Makes about 16.

CROQUE MONSIEUR (FRENCH TOASTED HAM AND CHEESE SANDWICH)

Preparation Time: 5 minutes
Cooking Time: 8 minutes

Prepare 2 ham-and-cheese sandwiches on mustard-spread French or white bread. Beat 1 egg lightly with ½ cup milk and ¼ teaspoon salt. Dip both sides of each sandwich in egg-and-milk mixture. Brown sandwiches on both sides in butter in hot skillet.
Makes 2 servings.

CROQUE MADAME

Prepare sandwiches as for Croque Monsieur, using sliced chicken in place of ham.

CROQUE MADEMOISELLE

Prepare sandwiches as for Croque Monsieur using cooked or canned asparagus in place of ham.

CURRIED EGGS

Preparation Time: 5 minutes
Cooking Time: 21 minutes

4 *eggs*
⅓ *cup mayonnaise*
2 *tablespoons sour cream*

1 *teaspoon curry powder*
Salt, pepper
Chives, chopped

Hard-cook 4 eggs. Meanwhile, stir mayonnaise with sour cream and curry powder. Chill and peel eggs, slice. Combine with sauce, adjust seasoning. Top with sprinkling of chives.
Makes 2 servings.

EGGS BENEDICT

Preparation Time: 8 minutes
Cooking Time: 5 minutes

4 *poached eggs*
2 *English muffins, split*
4 *small slices ham or can*
   (3 *ounces*) *deviled ham*

Hollandaise Sauce, Easy Way
   (*below*)

Poach eggs. Toast English Muffins. Cover each muffin with half slice of ham or spread with deviled ham. Top with poached egg, then with Hollandaise Sauce (page 134).
Makes 2 hearty servings.

HOLLANDAISE SAUCE, EASY WAY

Preparation Time: 3 minutes
Cooking Time: 5 to 7 minutes

Place stick of butter (¼ pound) in small cold skillet just as wide as the bar. Add 3 egg yolks, juice of ½ lemon, pinch of salt, dash of red pepper sauce. Cook over moderate heat, stirring constantly, until butter is melted and sauce thickens smoothly. That's all.

EGGS FOO YUNG

Preparation Time: 8 minutes
Cooking Time: 10 minutes

4 eggs
½ stalk celery, diced
1 green onion, diced
1 small can mushroom pieces

½ small green pepper, diced
Salt, pepper, fresh ginger
Peanut oil

Beat eggs light, add vegetables and seasonings, fold to blend. Heat peanut oil about ¼ inch deep in frying pan. When oil is hot, drop egg mixture by large spoonfuls into pan. Cook until golden brown on underside. Lower heat slightly and turn Foo Yung to brown other side. Serve with sauce below.
  Makes 2 to 3 servings.

  Note: Add diced cooked pork, chicken, shrimp; crabmeat or clams, if they are handy.

SAUCE

1 cup chicken broth
1 teaspoon sugar
1 tablespoon soy sauce

1 tablespoon cornstarch
¼ cup cold water

Combine broth, sugar and soy sauce, heat almost to boiling. Stir cornstarch to paste with cold water, add to broth mixture, and bring to a boil, stirring constantly. Continue to stir over heat until clear and thickened, adding a little hot water or sherry if sauce becomes too thick. Serve with Eggs Foo Yung and boiled rice, top with slivered almonds.

FONDUE

Preparation Time: 10 minutes
Cooking Time: 10 minutes

1 *clove garlic, halved*
1½ *cups white wine*
¾ *pound Gruyère cheese, diced*
2 *teaspoons cornstarch*

Dash of nutmeg
3 *tablespoons kirsch*
Pepper
½ *cup cream*
2 *egg yolks*

The fondue may be prepared in a chafing dish or in a heatproof casserole over low heat. Rub the dish with the cut clove of garlic. Add the wine and heat until bubbles begin to rise. Toss cheese with cornstarch, add to wine a handful at a time, stirring until the cheese melts. Add kirsch, stir to blend. Season with pepper to taste. Stir in cream and egg yolks. Serve with cubes of French bread, each with a bit of crust, through which bread is speared; and provide long-handled forks so that guests can dip the bread into the fondue.

Serves 8 to 12 as an appetizer, or 6 as a main dish for a light meal.

HUEVOS RANCHEROS

Preparation Time: 6 minutes
Cooking Time: 8 minutes

2 *tablespoons oil*
1 *small onion, diced*
½ *green pepper, diced*
1 *clove garlic, crushed*
1 *cup canned tomatoes with purée*

Salt, pepper, crumbled basil leaf
2 *to 4 eggs*

Heat oil; brown onion, pepper, garlic lightly, add tomatoes and seasonings. Cook, stirring, until blended. Make indents in sauce with back of spoon and drop eggs in. Cook until eggs are set, covering pan to set tops, if desired.

Makes 1 to 2 servings.

OMELET

Preparation Time: 2 minutes
Cooking Time: 1½ to 3 minutes

1 *teaspoon butter*   *Salt, pepper*
2 *eggs*
2 *tablespoons water, milk or*
   sour cream

Heat butter in 7-inch round-sided omelet pan reserved for this purpose. Beat eggs with liquid and seasonings, using a fork to beat just until light and bubbly. Pour into hot butter in pan. Reduce heat and cook, twisting pan occasionally back and forth over heat, and pulling egg in from sides to center as it sets, to allow liquid portion to run out to sides. As soon as top is set, flop one side over and roll out onto serving plate. Wipe pan with paper towel while it is still warm. If any egg sticks, rub with a little salt.

Makes 1 serving.

HERB OMELET

Add 1 tablespoon chopped fresh herbs to eggs before beating.

CHEESE OMELET

Sprinkle almost-set omelet with cheese of your choice before rolling.

Bacon Omelet

Cook bacon crisp, starting in cold pan. Crumble over almost-set egg before rolling.

Mushroom Omelet

Add browned mushrooms to top of almost-set omelet before rolling.

Red Caviar and Sour Cream Omelet

Top omelet with sour cream, red caviar and chives immediately after rolling onto platter.

Western Omelet

Chop 1 tablespoon each boiled ham, green pepper, onion, add to beaten egg before cooking.

Peasant Omelet

Sprinkle 4 tablespoons boiled diced potato, 2 tablespoons chopped onion over omelet as it sets.

RACLETTE

Preparation Time: 6 minutes
Cooking Time: 5 to 6 minutes

½ pound or 1 piece 4 x 8 x ½-inch Gruyère (or other semifirm cheese as Raclette, Tilsiter or Monterey Jack)

¼ teaspoon caraway seeds
½ teaspoon chopped parsley
Pepper
Sour pickles, onions

Place a stainless steel plate or pie pan on oven rack about 4 to 6 inches from heat. Heat plate about 5 minutes. Place cheese on hot plate and broil 5 to 6 minutes, or until cheese melts and is hot and bubbly. Remove from oven and sprinkle with caraway

seeds, parsley, and pepper. Garnish with sour pickles and onions, and serve from pan, with glasses of chilled beer.
Makes 2 servings.

SHIRRED EGGS FLORENTINE

Preparation Time: 6 minutes
Cooking Time: 12 minutes

½ *cup chopped cooked spinach*	1 *or 2 eggs*
Salt and pepper	*Grated cheese*
Dash of nutmeg	*Butter*
2 *tablespoons cream*	*Bread crumbs*
	Paprika

Preheat oven to 350° F. Place spinach in buttered ramekin or individual baking dish, add seasonings and cream. Make a hollow in spinach with back of spoon, and break egg in. Sprinkle with grated cheese. Dot top with butter, sprinkle lightly with bread crumbs and dash of paprika. Bake in a moderate oven about 12 minutes, until eggs are set.
Makes 1 serving.

WELSH RAREBIT

Preparation Time: 5 minutes
Cooking Time: 12 minutes

½ *pound Cheddar cheese*	¼ *teaspoon dry mustard*
1 *tablespoon butter*	1 *teaspoon Worcestershire sauce*
¼ *teaspoon salt*	¼ *cup ale or beer*
¼ *teaspoon paprika*	

Dice cheese and place in double boiler or chafing dish over low heat with butter. Combine all seasonings with ale. As cheese melts, add the ale mixture, stirring slowly and constantly until cheese is hot and bubbling. Serve on toast or crackers.
Makes 2 to 3 servings.

10 *Pasta and Rice and Grains*

These are the roundings-out, the satiety-makers, and the economical, nutritional meal balancers. While we tend to think of meat *and* pilaf or pasta or rice, the meat animal, particularly beef, is actually an inefficient machine for converting protein in grains to protein in muscle. Some of the dishes in this chapter are complete main dishes, and if you treat them as such, without additional meat and with only salad or fruit to round out the meal, you will keep calories as well as costs in trim.

While vegetable and grain proteins are not as complete as animal proteins, lacking in some of the essential amino acids, they may be utilized as complete when they are properly combined. This is particularly true when they are enjoyed together with some animal protein, as in macaroni with cheese, cereal with milk, buckwheat with egg or small amounts of fish or poultry or meat. Cereal combinations such as wheat with corn or rice, or any switch of the combinations above, provide good protein balance, at practical cost in time *and* money.

For better time saving still, cook ahead when there is time. Leftover boiled rice becomes Chinese fried rice, buckwheat makes the base of a tasty casserole, and pastas reincarnate in dishes from soups to casseroles or skillet meals. Pastas and grains tossed with French dressing or mayonnaise make marvelous hearty main-dish salads.

Don't waste any of the flavorful residue of cooking grains.

139

Instead of scrubbing the bits and pieces from the pan, boil them up with a little water and add to a refrigerator stock jar for soups. Or, toast rice left in the cooking pan over low heat until any rice left on the bottom dries in a cake which lifts off easily. Store in refrigerator, to drop into your next hot soup, or nibble it as a kitchen treat, Chinese style.

BROWN RICE

Preparation Time: 5 minutes in A.M.
Cooking Time: 5 minutes to reheat

1 *cup brown rice*
3 *cups boiling water*

1 *teaspoon salt*
2 *tablespoons butter*

In the morning, combine rice and salted boiling water in a pot with a tightly fitting lid and return to boil. Remove from heat and let stand on the back of the range until dinnertime. Reheat, toss with butter.

Makes 4 servings.

BULGUR PILAF

Preparation Time: 5 minutes
Cooking Time: 16 minutes

¼ *cup butter or oil*
1 *onion, chopped*
½ *cup chopped fresh mushrooms* (*or canned*)

1 *cup bulgur* (*wheat*)
2 *cups bouillon*
Salt, pepper

Heat butter and cook onion until lightly browned; add mushrooms. Add bulgur, stir for a moment to coat grains thoroughly. Add bouillon (made with cubes), bring to a boil, adjust seasoning, cover, simmer 14 minutes. Serve as accompaniment to meat, especially shish kebab.

Makes 4 to 6 servings.

BUCKWHEAT GROATS (KASHA)

Preparation Time: 5 minutes
Cooking Time: 16 minutes

1 cup whole buckwheat groats
1 egg
4 tablespoons butter or oil

1 onion, diced
2 cups boiling water or broth
Salt, pepper

Rinse buckwheat groats, heat in pan until dry. Beat egg lightly with fork, pour over groats, and cook, stirring, until kernels are browned and separate. Add butter or oil and diced onion and cook to glaze onion. Add water or broth, salt, pepper. Cover, simmer 14 minutes. To extend groats for hearty servings, add 1 can (12 ounces) vacuum-packed whole-kernel corn, stir and heat through.

Makes 4 to 6 servings.

CHICK-PEA CASSEROLE

Preparation Time: 4 minutes
Cooking Time: 23 minutes

1 pound sausage meat
1 tablespoon butter
1 onion, chopped
1 can (8 ounces) tomato sauce
1 tablespoon chopped parsley

¼ teaspoon oregano
¼ teaspoon basil
Salt, pepper
1 can (1 pound) chick-peas, drained

Shape sausage meat into small patties and brown slowly on both sides in butter. Add onion and cook until transparent. Add remaining ingredients, bring to a boil, cover, simmer 15 minutes. Serve with hot cooked green noodles.

Makes 4 to 6 servings.

FETTUCINI ALFREDO

Preparation Time: 5 minutes
Cooking Time: 6 minutes

8 *ounces medium noodles*   Pepper
¼ *pound butter, slivered*
1 *cup grated Parmesan cheese*

Cook noodles in boiling salted water until just tender, about 6 minutes. Drain and turn at once into a heated serving dish. Add butter, cheese and a generous amount of pepper and toss quickly until butter melts.
Makes 4 servings.

Variation: Substitute ½ cup warmed heavy cream for half the butter.

MACARONI AND CHEESE

Preparation Time: 5 minutes
Cooking Time: 14 to 20 minutes

8 *ounces macaroni*   ½ *pound Cheddar cheese,*
4 *tablespoons butter*   *shredded*
4 *tablespoons flour*   *Salt, pepper*
2 *cups milk*   ¾ *cup buttered bread crumbs*

Cook macaroni according to package directions until just tender. Meanwhile, melt butter, stir in flour and gradually add milk, stirring constantly until sauce is thickened and smooth. Stir in shredded cheese and salt and pepper to taste. When cheese melts, combine sauce with cooked, drained macaroni. Divide into 4 to 6 buttered individual baking dishes, or place in a shallow casserole. Sprinkle with buttered bread crumbs and brown under the broiler or in a very hot oven.
Makes 4 servings.

Variations: Add diced leftover ham, chicken, turkey or fish.

POLENTA

Preparation Time: 5 minutes
Cooking Time: 25 minutes

1 *cup cornmeal*
1 *cup cold water*
3 *cups boiling water*
1 *teaspoon salt*
2 *tablespoons butter*

Mushroom Tomato Sauce
  (see page 146)
Grated Parmesan cheese for
  topping

Stir cornmeal with cold water. Add to boiling water, stirring constantly until smooth and thickened. Cook over very low heat, or in double boiler, covered, stirring occasionally, for 15 to 20 minutes longer. Add butter. Cover with Mushroom Tomato Sauce (page 146) or any desired spaghetti sauce and top with grated Parmesan.

MAMALIGA

Cook cornmeal as above; instead of sauce serve with cottage cheese and sour cream for a mid-European alternate to polenta. It's a curiously satisfying bland flavor combination for a light supper.

RICE PILAF

Preparation Time: 3 minutes
Cooking Time: 17 minutes

2 *tablespoons butter*
1 *small onion, chopped*
1 *cup rice*

2 *cups bouillon or water*
Pepper

Melt butter, cook onion until lightly golden. Add rice, stir to coat grains thoroughly. Add bouillon or water, bring to a boil, cover, simmer 14 minutes until rice is tender, dry and fluffy.
Makes 3 to 4 servings.

ORIENTAL PILAF

Add rice to butter and onions as for Rice Pilaf. Add 2 cups water with a piece of stick cinnamon and ½ cup raisins or currants, and bring to boil. Cook rice until tender. Discard cinnamon, add ½ cup slivered almonds, toss and serve.

RISOTTO

Top pilaf cooked with bouillon with ¼ cup grated Parmesan cheese.

RISI BISI

Toss hot risotto with 1 can (1 pound) drained peas.

RISOTTO MILANESE

Add to risotto ¼ pound sliced chicken livers, browned in butter; or 1 cup sliced mushrooms, browned in butter; add a pinch of saffron to the cooking water, plus 2 tablespoons wine. Cook as directed.

SPAGHETTI

Preparation Time: 6 minutes
Cooking Time: 7 to 10 minutes

Allow ½ pound spaghetti to serve 4 as a main dish. Bring 2 quarts of water to a boil with 2 teaspoons salt; add a tablespoon of oil. Boil spaghetti 7 to 10 minutes until it is just tender; cut a strand with a knife to make sure that it does not have a dry, hard center. Drain and toss with sauce, which you can prepare while the spaghetti cooks.

Carbonara Sauce

Preparation Time: 3 minutes
Cooking Time: 4 minutes

¼ pound lean bacon strips
Butter
2 hard-cooked eggs, chopped

1 teaspoon coarsely ground
black pepper
Grated Romano cheese

Sauté bacon in butter until crisp; crumble bacon and return it to pan drippings with eggs and black pepper. Toss with cooked spaghetti. Add cheese.
Makes 4 servings.

Clam Sauce

Preparation Time: 2 minutes
Cooking Time: 5 minutes

2 cloves garlic, minced
¼ cup oil
1 can (8 to 10 ounces) minced
clams

2 tablespoons chopped parsley

Sauté garlic in oil until golden. Add juice drained from clams, simmer 2 minutes. Add clams and parsley, heat through. Toss with hot cooked spaghetti.
Makes 4 servings.

Variations: Add a small can of cooked shrimp to the clam sauce; or use oysters instead of clams.

Green Sauce

Preparation Time: 3 minutes
Cooking Time: 5 minutes

1 clove garlic
⅓ cup oil
¾ cup finely chopped parsley

1 teaspoon dried basil
Salt, pepper

Sauté garlic in oil until golden. Add remaining ingredients and heat for a minute or two. Toss with hot cooked spaghetti.
Makes 4 servings.

MUSHROOM TOMATO SAUCE

Preparation Time: 4 minutes
Cooking Time: 25 minutes

¼ cup olive oil
1 onion, chopped
1 garlic clove, minced
¼ pound mushrooms (or 2-ounce can)

1 can (1 pound 4 ounces) tomatoes, mashed
1 can (6 ounces) tomato paste

Brown onion, garlic and mushrooms in hot oil; add remaining ingredients, including liquid drained from mushrooms, bring to a boil and simmer about 20 minutes, or longer for a thicker sauce.
Makes 4 servings.

SAUSAGE TOMATO SAUCE

Reduce oil to 2 tablespoons and brown ½ to 1 pound Italian sausage, sliced, with onion and garlic as in Mushroom Tomato Sauce, above. Pour off half the drippings before adding the tomatoes and tomato paste and simmer as above.
Makes 4 servings.

SPATZLE

Preparation Time: 8 minutes
Cooking Time: 12 minutes

3 quarts water
1 teaspoon salt
1½ cups flour
½ teaspoon salt

Pepper, nutmeg
2 eggs
½ cup milk or broth
¼ cup butter

Put salted water on high heat to boil, covered. Meanwhile, combine flour and seasonings. Beat eggs and milk or broth. Add gradually to flour to make a thick batter. Beat well. Pour about ¾ cup of the batter into a colander with large holes, directly over the boiling water, so the batter can drip through. The *spätzle* will puff and rise to the top in about 5 minutes. Cook for a minute longer and remove with a slotted spoon, draining well. Repeat until all the batter is used. Melt butter in a skillet, add *spätzle*, and reheat briefly. Serve instead of potatoes or rice—especially good with stews.

Makes 4 to 6 servings.

11 New and Varied Vegetable Dishes

The pleasure of greeting spring with asparagus, summer with sun-sweetened corn, autumn with hearty golden squash, a winter party with Brussels sprouts and chestnuts, is still especially satisfying, even though you can now enjoy all these things any time of the year. While out-of-season vegetables have their own unique pleasures, and frozen and canned fill out menus, watch the vegetable stands for the seasonal flow that offers fast cooking, best price for the pleasure of fresh and tender produce.

For me, the best way to cook vegetables is as briefly as possible. I heat a little oil in a skillet, add cleaned and cut vegetables, season with salt, pepper, sometimes nutmeg (when cooking spinach), ginger (for Chinese cabbage), caraway (for cabbage). Add snipped herbs, cover snugly and cook until barely tender, or toss in open skillet or wok to stir-fry quickly.

Mixtures of vegetables are too good to leave to the frozen-food manufacturers; make your own combinations in minutes. Add a dash of soy sauce for Chinese flavor, particularly with greens; or a spoonful of spaghetti sauce for an Italian menu; sour cream for a Polish or Russian flavor; or paprika for Hungarian, dill and butter for Danish.

Leftover vegetables are your next day's pleasure, in sandwich, salad, soup or casserole. Those qualities of good nutritional value, from vitamins to minerals, become *your* vitality, vim, and vigor.

ARTICHOKE HEARTS

Preparation Time: 5 minutes
Cooking Time: 14 minutes

3 tablespoons olive oil
1 shallot or scallion finely
   chopped
1 package (10 ounces) frozen
   hearts

¼ teaspoon basil
Salt

Heat olive oil in a medium skillet. Add shallot or scallion and sauté 1 minute. Add artichoke hearts and seasonings and cook, stirring occasionally, until artichoke hearts are just tender, about 10 minutes. Serve immediately.
Makes 3 to 4 servings.

ASPARAGUS HOLLANDAISE

Preparation Time: 5 minutes
Cooking Time: 15 minutes

1 pound fresh asparagus
Salt

⅔ cup Hollandaise Sauce,
   Easy Way (recipe page 134)

Scrub asparagus stalks well and snap to break off tough lower ends. Bring to boiling salted water 3 to 4 inches deep in a straight-sided coffeepot or the top of a double boiler. Tie asparagus together in a bunch and place in the boiling water. Cover with top of coffeepot or inverted bottom of double boiler. Steam until tender, about 12 minutes. Meanwhile, prepare Hollandaise sauce. Remove string and serve asparagus with sauce.
Makes 2 servings.

Note: For a quicker topping use ½ cup melted butter and serve with fresh lemon wedges.

BRAISED LEEKS

Preparation Time: 4 minutes
Cooking Time: 15 minutes

6 leeks
2 tablespoons butter
1 to 1½ cups chicken broth

Salt and pepper
Fresh chopped parsley (optional)

Cut off the tops of the leeks an inch or two above the point where the color changes. Cut in half lengthwise and wash thoroughly. In medium skillet melt butter. Add leeks, cut side down, and cover with the chicken broth. Season to taste; cover and simmer until the leeks are just tender, 12 to 15 minutes. Serve in individual au gratin dishes with the broth or serve broth separately in cups. Top with chopped parsley, if desired.
Makes 3 to 4 servings.

BROCCOLI

Preparation Time: 5 minutes
Cooking Time: 14 minutes

1 bunch fresh broccoli
2 tablespoons oil
1 cup boiling water

Salt
¼ cup shredded Cheddar cheese (optional)

Cut away tough stems and wash broccoli. Cut large stalks in strips. In large skillet, heat oil. Add the broccoli. Add water and salt, cover. Cook until broccoli is just tender, about 10 minutes. Top with cheese, if desired, and turn into a serving dish. Serve immediately.
Makes 4 servings.

BRUSSELS SPROUTS WITH CHESTNUTS

Preparation Time: 3 minutes
Cooking Time: 19 minutes

3 packages (10 ounces) frozen
  Brussels sprouts
1 can (1 pound 4 ounces)
  chestnuts in syrup

2 tablespoons butter
Dash of nutmeg
Salt and pepper

Cook Brussels sprouts according to package directions. Drain chestnuts, reserving ¼ cup of their liquid. When Brussels sprouts are done drain and set aside. Heat butter, chestnuts, and reserved liquid until slightly caramelized. Add sprouts and simmer 5 minutes. Dust with nutmeg and season with salt and pepper to taste.
Makes 10 to 12 servings.

CABBAGE PARMESAN

Preparation Time: 6 minutes
Cooking Time: 9 minutes

½ medium head cabbage
  (about 1 pound)
1 small onion, diced
2 tablespoons butter or margarine

1 tablespoon salt
Pepper
⅓ cup grated Parmesan cheese

Wash and quickly shred cabbage with a sharp knife; dice onion. In a very large skillet heat butter or margarine and sauté cabbage and onion just until tender-crisp. Sprinkle with salt, pepper and Parmesan cheese; mix until well combined. Serve immediately.
Makes 3 servings.

CANDIED YAMS

Preparation Time: 4 minutes
Cooking Time: 6 minutes

1 can (16 ounces) yams
¼ cup apricot preserves

1 tablespoon chopped pecans

Heat yams according to package directions. Drain and toss in the apricot preserves. Remove to a serving dish and top with chopped pecans.

Makes 2 to 3 servings.

CARROTS A L'ORANGE

Preparation Time: 8 minutes
Cooking Time: 12 minutes

1 pound carrots, peeled and
    cut into ⅛-inch slices
¾ cup orange juice
1½ teaspoons sugar
Salt

Ground ginger
1 tablespoon butter
2 oranges, peeled, cut in
    wedges

Simmer carrots in orange juice with seasonings and butter until tender, about 10 minutes. Add orange wedges and heat through.

Makes 4 servings.

CHINESE-STYLE VEGETABLES

Preparation Time: 12 minutes
Cooking Time: 8 minutes

¼ cup salad oil
4 scallions, sliced
¼ pound fresh mushrooms, sliced
½ head Chinese cabbage, sliced
1 green pepper, sliced into strips

1 can (6 ounces) water chestnuts, sliced
1 cup fresh or canned bean sprouts, drained
1 pimento, chopped
3 tablespoons soy sauce
1 tablespoon cornstarch
1 tablespoon sherry

Wash and prepare vegetables first. In very large skillet, heat oil and sauté scallions and mushrooms until just tender; add cabbage and green pepper and cook over high heat, stirring constantly until cabbage is just tender, about 5 minutes. Add water chestnuts, bean sprouts, and pimento and cook until heated through. Stir soy sauce with cornstarch and sherry and add to pan. Return to boil. Serve immediately.

Makes 6 servings.

CORN ON THE COB

Preparation Time: 8 minutes
Cooking Time: 5 minutes

The secret of good corn is quick cooking after husking. Avoid pre-husked corn.

2 quarts water
Salt

6 ears corn
Butter

In a large kettle heat to boiling 2 quarts of salted water. Meanwhile, husk the corn and cut off the stems. Add some of inner husks to water. When the water boils, add the corn and cook 5 minutes. Serve immediately with salt and melted butter.

Makes 3 to 6 servings.

CORN OYSTERS

Preparation Time: 7 minutes
Cooking Time: 6 minutes

1 can (12 ounces) yellow corn
   kernels
2 eggs
1 tablespoon flour

½ teaspoon dried onion flakes
¼ teaspoon salt
Pepper to taste
Oil or butter

Drain corn. In a medium bowl combine the eggs, flour, onion, salt and pepper until well mixed. Stir in drained corn. Drop by tablespoonfuls onto hot buttered or oiled skillet. Brown on both sides and remove to serving plate. Keep warm until serving. Pass syrup or honey for topping.

Makes 4 servings.

EGGPLANT MOZZARELLA

Preparation Time: 8 minutes
Cooking Time: 20 minutes

¾ cup flour
Salt and pepper
1 eggplant, sliced
¼ cup melted butter or ¼ cup
   oil
2 large tomatoes, sliced or 1
   can (16 ounces) tomatoes

1 large onion, thinly sliced
½ cup grated mozzarella
   cheese
2 tablespoons Parmesan cheese
¼ teaspoon oregano

Preheat oven to 500° F. Mix flour and salt and pepper in a medium-sized plastic bag. Brush eggplant slices with some of the butter or oil and toss them in the flour. Shake off excess flour. Brown the slices quickly in remaining butter or oil in a very large skillet or electric fry pan, removing slices to 2-quart casserole as they finish. Alternate eggplant slices and tomato in casserole. Sauté onion in skillet with last pieces of eggplant and arrange over the eggplant and tomato slices. Top with cheeses and oregano. Place in hot oven until eggplant is tender and cheese is melted, about 5 minutes.

Makes 4 servings.

FRIED POTATOES PARMESAN

Preparation Time: 4 minutes
Cooking Time: 20 minutes

3 tablespoons butter
2 large potatoes, sliced in ¼-inch-thick slices

Salt
3 tablespoons grated Parmesan cheese

Heat butter in a large skillet or electric fry pan. Sauté potatoes in butter until golden. Turn; lower heat and sauté, covered, for 8 to 10 minutes or until just tender. Season to taste, sprinkle with cheese and sauté, covered, another 5 minutes.

Makes 2 to 3 servings.

GOLDEN BEAN BAKE

Preparation Time: 7 minutes
Cooking Time: 15 minutes

2 cans (16 ounces each) New England style baked beans
3 tablespoons orange marmalade or molasses
3 tablespoons prepared mustard

1 tablespoon instant minced onion
¼ cup (½ stick) butter or margarine, softened
1 tablespoon prepared mustard
6 slices fresh French bread

Preheat oven to 450° F. In a 1-quart casserole combine beans, marmalade, the 3 tablespoons mustard, and onion. Bake 10 minutes. Meanwhile, blend together the butter and 1 tablespoon mustard and spread on the bread. Remove casserole from the oven and arrange bread slices around the edges to form an overlapping pattern. Bake 5 minutes longer. Serve beans over toasted bread slices.

Makes 4 to 6 servings.

Note: This makes a perfect quick luncheon dish with a green salad and a fruit dessert.

GREEN BEANS AND MUSHROOMS PIQUANT

Preparation Time: 6 minutes
Cooking Time: 16 minutes

¼ *pound fresh mushrooms, washed and sliced*
1 *tablespoon butter*
1 *package (10 ounces) frozen green beans*
1 *package (3 ounces) cream cheese*
⅛ *teaspoon chili powder*
½ *teaspoon paprika*
1 *tablespoon capers*

In small skillet sauté mushrooms in butter until golden. Add green beans and ½ cup water and cook according to package directions. Meanwhile, stir together cream cheese, chili powder, paprika and capers until cream cheese is softened and capers are mashed. When beans are tender, remove from heat and measure ⅓ cup of the hot liquid from them. Drain and discard any excess liquid. Gradually stir the hot liquid into the cream cheese mixture and pour it over the hot vegetables. Stir until well combined and serve immediately.

Makes 4 servings.

MUSHROOMS IN CREAM

Preparation Time: 6 minutes
Cooking Time: 10 minutes

1 *pound fresh mushrooms,*
washed and halved
2 *tablespoons butter*

1 *single serving packet instant*
onion-soup mix
½ *cup sour cream*

In a large skillet sauté mushrooms until tender. Stir in soup mix and stir until well combined. Add sour cream and heat, stirring, until just hot. Serve immediately.
Makes 4 to 6 servings.

ONIONS A LA MADRID

Preparation Time: 8 minutes
Cooking Time: 15 minutes

1 *or 2 medium-large sweet*
Spanish onions, sliced and
separated into rings
1 *tablespoon butter or marga-*
rine
⅓ *cup mayonnaise*
2 *tablespoons Worcestershire*
sauce

2 *tablespoons slivered almonds*
1 *pimento, cut into strips*
¼ *cup flour*
¼ *cup grated Parmesan cheese*
1 *tablespoon chopped parsley*
1 *tablespoon mayonnaise*

Preheat oven to 400° F. In small ovenproof skillet sauté onion rings in butter until just tender. Remove from heat and stir in the ⅓ cup mayonnaise, Worcestershire sauce, almonds and pimento all at once. In a small bowl mix together flour, cheese, parsley, and 1 tablespoon mayonnaise with a fork until well combined. Spread over onions and bake until topping is golden, about 10 minutes.
Makes 2 servings.

PARSLEYED BOILED POTATOES

Preparation Time: 5 minutes
Cooking Time: 12 minutes

Small new potatoes
Water
Salt

Butter
Snipped parsley

Set pan to boil with water 1 inch deep. Meanwhile, wash new potatoes and cut in quarters, without peeling, cutting away any bruised spots. Rinse, then drop into water. Add salt. Cover, boil about 8 minutes, until tender. If water hasn't cooked away, uncover pan and cook a few minutes longer, shaking potatoes dry in pan. Add butter and parsley, turning to coat. Serve, spooning pan sauce over.

PEAS BONNE FEMME

Preparation Time: 3 minutes
Cooking Time: 8 minutes

2 scallions, sliced
2 tablespoons butter or margarine
1 package (10 ounces) frozen peas

½ teaspoon salt
2 or 3 iceberg or Boston lettuce leaves

In small saucepan sauté scallions in butter over medium heat just until golden. Add peas, the frozen block broken up as much as possible. Sprinkle with salt. Cover with lettuce leaves; lower heat, cover pot with tight lid and allow to steam until peas are just tender, 6 to 8 minutes—uncover and stir once during cooking, replacing lettuce leaves after stirring.
Makes 4 servings.

POTATO-CHEESE BAKE

Preparation Time: 8 minutes
Cooking Time: 20 minutes

1 *can* (10¼ *ounces*) *condensed cream of potato soup, undiluted*
2 *cans* (16 *ounces each*) *potatoes*

1 *package* (8 *ounces*) *American cheese slices*
¼ *cup chopped salted peanuts*

Preheat oven to 400° F. In small saucepan heat soup to boiling, stirring frequently. In medium casserole make 3 layers, 1 layer each of potatoes, sauce and cheese, ending with cheese. Bake 10 minutes. Top with peanuts and return to oven for another 5 minutes.

Makes 6 servings.

POTATO PANCAKES

Preparation Time: 5 minutes
Cooking Time: 12 minutes

2 *large or 4 medium potatoes, peeled and coarsely cut*
1 *small onion, coarsely chopped*

2 *eggs*
2 *tablespoons flour*
1 *teaspoon salt*
Butter or oil

Put half the potatoes into the container of your blender with cold water to cover. Cover, blend 4 seconds, until grated. Remove to a sieve and drain. Repeat with the remainder. Blend onion with eggs. Add to grated potato. Stir in flour and salt. Drop by tablespoonfuls into hot fat in a large skillet. Brown on both sides. Serve hot with applesauce and/or sausages.

Makes 4 servings.

POTATOES ROESTI

Preparation Time: 5 minutes
Cooking Time: 15 minutes

2 potatoes, peeled, in large dice   ¼ teaspoon salt
3 tablespoons butter   Dash of pepper

Parboil potatoes 5 minutes. Drain. Place half the potatoes in blender container and cover. Coarse-chop 7 seconds. Remove, repeat with remaining potatoes. Melt butter in 9- or 10-inch skillet. Add potatoes and cook without stirring over very low heat until potatoes are tender and crispy brown on bottom. Season. Turn carefully, pancake style, and quickly brown other side.

Makes 2 to 3 servings.

POTATO SLICES, BROILED

Preparation Time: 2 minutes per potato
Cooking Time: 10 minutes

Peel potatoes (½ medium-sized potato per person). Cut in ¼-inch slices, brush lightly with oil or butter (dieters dip in cold water instead). Sprinkle with salt and paprika. Broil on rack 3 inches from heat, 5 minutes each side.

RATATOUILLE

Preparation Time: 10 minutes
Cooking Time: 18 minutes

1 *large onion, coarsely chopped*
1 *clove garlic, pressed*
¼ *cup salad oil or olive oil*
½ *pound mushrooms, sliced*
1 *green pepper, cut into squares*
1 *medium eggplant, peeled and cubed*

2 *zucchini, sliced*
2 *large tomatoes, quartered or* 1 *can* (18 *ounces*) *tomatoes*
½ *teaspoon oregano*
Salt and pepper

In a large skillet, over high heat, sauté onion and garlic in oil 1 minute. Stir in mushrooms and green pepper; sauté another 2 minutes. Stir in eggplant, zucchini, tomatoes, oregano and salt and pepper to taste. Cover and lower heat; cook 15 minutes, stirring occasionally.

Makes 6 to 8 servings.

RED CABBAGE WITH APPLE

Preparation Time: 7 minutes
Cooking Time: 23 minutes

1 *small head red cabbage*
1 *tart apple*
1 *strip bacon cut up*
1 *or* 2 *tablespoons oil*
1 *small onion, finely chopped*
Salt and pepper

¾ *cup water*
½ *cup red table wine*
¼ *cup cider vinegar*
2 *tablespoons sugar*
1 *tablespoon flour*

Wash and shred the red cabbage. Wash the apple, core and slice; do not peel. In a large skillet sauté the bacon until done. Add the cabbage, apple, and onion to the fat. Stir to glaze. Season well with salt and pepper. Add water and wine. Cover and simmer until cabbage is just tender. Stir together vinegar, sugar and flour. Add to cabbage. Stir until smooth. Cook over medium heat until thickened.

Makes 4 to 5 servings.

Spinach and Variations

BASIC COOKED SPINACH

Preparation Time: 5 minutes
Cooking Time: 5 minutes

1 *pound fresh spinach (or 10-*   Salt
  ounce bag, cleaned)   Nutmeg or soy sauce
1 *tablespoon oil*

Wash spinach thoroughly, lifting out of cold water until water is clear. Trim stems. Place oil in skillet or pan, add spinach with water which clings to the leaves. Add salt and dash nutmeg or soy sauce, to taste. Cover, simmer until just tender, 5 minutes. Spoon onto serving plate. Add butter or a little cream, if desired; or use in one of the 3 following recipes. (Reserve any cooking liquor or leftover spinach for the soup pot or to combine with rice or leftover mashed potatoes.)

Makes 3 servings.

SPINACH WITH SOUR CREAM

Preparation Time: 3 minutes
Cooking Time: 5 minutes

In a small bowl mix together ¼ cup sour cream, ¼ teaspoon salt, and ⅛ teaspoon nutmeg, and 1 tablespoon flour. Add to drained Basic Cooked Spinach, above, and heat, stirring, until mixture is hot. Serve immediately.

Makes 4 servings.

SPINACH WITH GARLIC BUTTER

Preparation Time: 6 minutes
Cooking Time: 6 minutes

Drain cooked spinach (see Basic Cooked Spinach, page 162) thoroughly. Toss with 3 tablespoons melted butter and 1 small clove garlic, pressed.
Makes 2 servings.

SPINACH WITH CHEESE

Preparation Time: 12 minutes
Cooking Time: 8 minutes

Cook 2 pounds spinach as in Basic Cooked Spinach. In a small bowl, beat 1 package (3 ounces) cream cheese or ½ cup ricotta, 1 egg, 2 tablespoons milk and ¼ teaspoon salt. Drain and chop the spinach. Sauté 1 small onion, chopped, in 1 tablespoon butter until it is golden. Stir in spinach and cheese mixture until well combined. Serve immediately.
Makes 6 to 8 servings.

STUFFED MUSHROOMS

Preparation Time: 10 minutes
Cooking Time: 12 minutes

1 *pound uniformly medium-size mushrooms*
2 *tablespoons Worcestershire sauce*
4 *tablespoons sherry*
½ *teaspoon dried parsley flakes*

4 *tablespoons (2 ounces) liver pâté or finely chopped left-over meat or chicken*
2 *tablespoons butter*

Wash and stem mushrooms. Set oven to preheat to 400° F. Chop stems finely and place in a small bowl along with the Worcestershire sauce, 2 tablespoons sherry, parsley and liver pâté or meat. Stir until well combined. Fill hollows of mushrooms with the mixture. Place in well-buttered baking dish. Add remaining tablespoons sherry to the pan and bake 12 minutes. Spoon sauce over and serve.

Makes 4 to 6 servings.

SWEET-AND-SOUR BEETS AND ONIONS

Preparation Time: 3 minutes
Cooking Time: 12 minutes

1 can (16 ounces) baby whole beets
1 can (16 ounces) small whole onions
½ cup sugar

¼ cup cider vinegar
1 tablespoon cornstarch
⅛ teaspoon cinnamon
1 tablespoon butter

Drain beets, reserving ½ cup of the juice. Drain onions, discard the juice. In a medium saucepan combine the beet juice, sugar, vinegar, cornstarch, cinnamon and butter. Stir with a wire whisk until well combined. Bring to boiling over medium heat, stirring until thickened. Add beets and onions and heat until they are warmed through, about 5 minutes, or until serving.

Makes 6 servings.

TOMATO AND ONION BROIL

Preparation Time: 8 minutes
Cooking Time: 8 to 10 minutes

¼ cup melted butter
¼ teaspoon basil
Salt and pepper
2 large Bermuda onions, cut into thick slices

2 large, firm tomatoes, cut into thick slices

Preheat broiler. Combine butter, basil, and salt and pepper to taste. Arrange onions on broiler pan and brush with some of the butter. Place under broiler and broil until onions are golden, 3 minutes. Remove from broiler and turn onions. Arrange tomato slices on broiler pan; brush all with butter mixture and broil another 3 minutes. Turn tomato slices and brush with remaining butter mixture; broil until onions are just tender. If ingredients get brown before they are quite tender lower broiler pan for the last few minutes.

Makes 4 servings.

VEGETABLE SAUCES

Simple sauces add greatly to the flavor and appeal of vegetables. Choose the flavor that sets off the main dish as well as the vegetable to best advantage.

AMANDINE

Brown slivered blanched almonds lightly in butter; salt and add with butter to vegetables. Great with green beans and fish.

LEMON BUTTER

Melt butter or margarine and add an equal amount of lemon juice. Excellent with broccoli.

SOUR CREAM DILL SAUCE

Combine 1 cup sour cream, ¼ teaspoon salt, 1 teaspoon chopped onions and ¼ cup finely chopped fresh dill or 1 tablespoon dry dill weed. Serve with mixed vegetables, cold meats or fish dishes.

CHIVE SAUCE

Combine ½ cup plain yogurt, 2 tablespoons snipped fresh chives, dash salt. Use to top potatoes.

VEGETABLES WITH CHEESE

Preparation Time: 5 minutes
Cooking Time: 10 minutes

2 packages (10 ounces each) frozen mixed vegetables
¾ cup milk

2 tablespoons flour
Salt and pepper
½ cup grated cheese

Prepare frozen vegetables according to package directions. Meanwhile in small saucepan stir together milk, flour and salt and pepper to taste, with a wire whisk. Bring to boiling, stirring constantly; stir in cheese until smooth and set aside. When vegetables are cooked, drain well; pour sauce over them and mix until well combined. Serve immediately.

Makes 6 servings.

ZUCCHINI, BRAISED

Preparation Time: 4 minutes
Cooking Time: 6 minutes

2 zucchini
2 tablespoons oil
½ small onion

Salt, pepper, basil
3 tablespoons water

Wash zucchini, trim ends and slice. Heat oil, add onion, zucchini, seasoning and water. Cover and braise 5 minutes.

Makes 2 servings.

ZUCCHINI WITH RICE AND TOMATOES

Preparation Time: 6 minutes
Cooking Time: 16 minutes

1 cup water
Salt
½ cup rice
2 tablespoons butter
1 small garlic clove, pressed
½ cup cherry tomatoes, halved

3 zucchini, washed and sliced
¼ cup water
Salt, pepper
Oregano
Grated Parmesan cheese

In a medium saucepan bring to boiling 1 cup salted water and cook the rice until tender—14 minutes. Meanwhile melt the butter in large saucepan and sauté garlic several seconds. Add tomatoes and sauté 1 minute. Add zucchini and ¼ cup water. Season with salt and pepper, cover and cook 5 to 6 minutes, until tender. Add rice to tomato-zucchini mixture. Add a pinch of oregano. Mix until ingredients are well combined and turn into a serving dish. Top with Parmesan cheese.

Makes 4 to 6 servings.

12 *Salads—Star and Supporting Roles*

A good salad makes a fresh mealtime note for any course from appetizer to main dish or dessert. And salad is more than lettuce, lettuce more than iceberg! Choose crisp, oval-leaved Romaine, curly chicory, soft Boston or buttery Bibb (if you are lucky enough to find it), coarse and slightly bitter escarole. Trim tender young spinach leaves, tender tops of beets, celery tops, even tender leaves of Swiss chard, and store with the salad greens. When you bring your greens home, wash thoroughly, discard any bruised leaves, shake off excess water, then wrap in a thick terry towel or paper towels, and store in the refrigerator. Iceberg lettuce and Belgian endive are best trimmed and washed as used.

Cabbage, red and green, makes thrifty and delicious salads, especially in winter. Good additions to a salad are leftover cooked vegetables, cooked cold rice, a random apple, orange, or canned vegetables from bean sprouts to beets. Almost any vegetable, raw or cooked, may be tossed with French dressing as a salad. Zucchini, eggplant, and their combination as ratatouille, beets, beans, asparagus—you name it, for tasty salad additions. And don't overlook nuts, bits of cheese, dried fruits.

The market is full of prepared salad-dressing mixes, but they are never as good as dressings made from scratch. It takes 2 minutes even for a slow assembler to combine 2 or 3 parts oil or sour cream or yogurt with 1 part vinegar or wine or lemon

168

juice, and season to taste. It takes 3 minutes to make mayonnaise in the blender. These can be served up in the glass in which they are mixed or combined with the salad greens just before serving. (See recipes at end of this chapter.)

And if you have salad left over, enjoy the bonus by blending the ingredients, including the dressing, in a tangy soup. If you begin with greens, green pepper, tomatoes, cucumber, add tomato juice for a quick gazpacho; or use the blended ingredients as a tasty addition to any soup. The imaginative cook will find many other uses for stored salad ingredients.

AVOCADO SALAD

Preparation Time: 3 minutes
Cooking Time: None

1 *avocado*
Grapefruit sections or cooked shrimp or crab or jellied consommé

French dressing or lemon juice or mayonnaise

Choose a ripe avocado—or keep an avocado, perhaps in a fruit centerpiece on your table, until soft to the touch. Cut in half, horizontally. Split to release seed (save the seed, suspend in water by piercing with toothpicks, which rest on rim of glass, until it roots, then plant for a great house plant). Fill avocado halves with grapefruit sections or seafood or jellied consommé. Top with French dressing or lemon juice or mayonnaise.

Makes 2 servings.

BEAN SALAD, RED AND WHITE

Preparation Time: 7 minutes
Cooking Time: None

1 can (16 ounces) red kidney
beans, drained
1 can (16 ounces) cannellini
(white kidney beans),
drained

3 scallions, chopped
1 dill pickle, chopped
1 teaspoon fresh or dried
chopped parsley
¾ cup French dressing

In a medium-size bowl, toss together all ingredients until well combined. Refrigerate until serving.
Makes 6 servings.

BEET SALAD

Preparation Time: 8 minutes
Cooking Time: None

1 can (16 ounces) sliced beets
2 large oranges, peeled and
sliced
1 Bermuda onion, thinly
sliced

½ cup French dressing made
with lemon juice
2 tablespoons orange marmalade

Drain beets and arrange in shallow serving dish, alternating with orange slices and onion slices. Mix together dressing and marmalade and pour over beets, oranges and onions. Refrigerate until serving.
Makes 4 servings.

BLENDER COLE SLAW

Preparation Time: 12 minutes
Cooking Time: None

1 *small head cabbage*
½ *cup ice water*
1 *small carrot, peeled*
½ *onion, coarsely cut*
1 *green pepper, coarsely cut*

1 *teaspoon salt*
2 *tablespoons vinegar*
1 *tablespoon caraway seeds*
1 *or more cups sour cream to moisten*

Cut cabbage into wedges, then slice. Into container of blender put cabbage, 1 cup at a time, with ¼ cup ice water. Cover, blend about 2 seconds, until cabbage has been shredded. Remove. Repeat with remainder of cabbage and ice water. Remove. Blend carrot, onion and pepper to chop finely. Combine with drained cabbage. Add salt, vinegar, caraway seeds and sour cream; toss well to mix. Refrigerate until serving.

Makes 6 servings.

CAESAR SALAD

Preparation Time: 7 minutes
Cooking Time: 1 minute

1 *egg*
2 *heads romaine lettuce*
½ *cup crumbled Roquefort cheese*
2 *cups garlic croutons*

6 *anchovy fillets (optional)*
½ *cup oil-and-vinegar dressing*
1 *teaspoon Worcestershire sauce*
1 *tablespoon lemon juice*

In a small saucepan, bring to boil about 1 cup water; carefully place the egg into the boiling water and cook 1 minute. Remove and place in cool water. Meanwhile wash and drain romaine leaves. Break into bits in a large salad bowl, top with cheese, croutons, and cut-up anchovies if desired. In a small bowl beat together the coddled egg, oil-and-vinegar dressing, Worcestershire sauce and lemon juice. Pour over the salad and toss until greens are well coated.

Makes 4 to 6 servings.

CHEF'S SALAD BOWLS

Preparation Time: 12 minutes
Cooking Time: None

½ *head romaine lettuce*
½ *head Boston lettuce*
½ *cucumber, sliced unpeeled*
2 *tomatoes, cut into wedges*
2 *hard-cooked eggs, quartered*
4 *ounces boiled ham slices, cut into strips*

4 *ounces turkey loaf slices, cut into strips*
4 *ounces Cheddar cheese slices, cut into strips*

Wash and drain lettuces. Break into pieces in a large salad bowl or 4 small salad bowls. Arrange cucumber slices, tomatoes, egg, ham, turkey and cheese on top of the lettuce. Serve with ¼ to ⅓ cup of salad dressing (blue cheese, Green Goddess or French) per serving.

Makes 4 main-dish servings.

CLASSIC GREEN SALAD WITH HERBS

Preparation Time: 10 minutes
Cooking Time: None

1 *head romaine lettuce*
1 *head Boston lettuce*
1 *Belgian endive*
1 *bunch watercress*

1 *teaspoon chopped chives*
1 *teaspoon chopped fresh dill*
¾ *cup French dressing*

Wash and carefully dry all greens. Break lettuce and endive into a large salad bowl. Top with watercress, chives and dill. Chill until serving. At serving time toss with dressing until greens are well coated.

Makes 6 servings.

CUCUMBERS IN SOUR CREAM

Preparation Time: 6 minutes
Cooking Time: None

1 *large cucumber*
Salt
½ *cup sour cream*
1 *tablespoon cider vinegar*

¼ *teaspoon dried dill weed*
Pepper
Salad greens

Peel and slice cucumber, add salt and let stand. In medium-size bowl, combine sour cream, vinegar, dill weed, and pepper to taste. Drain cucumber slices, add sour cream mixture, and toss until they are well coated. Arrange on salad greens and serve immediately.

Makes 4 servings.

Note: For a main-dish salad add one jar (8 ounces) herring in cream.

FRENCH GREEN SALAD WITH
BEETS AND NUTS

Preparation Time: 8 minutes
Cooking Time: None

1 *head romaine lettuce*
Few spinach leaves (optional)
½ *cup julienne-cut canned beets*

¼ *cup walnut halves*
1 *teaspoon finely chopped fresh tarragon (optional)*
½ *cup French dressing*

Wash and carefully drain greens, break into salad bowl. Top with beets, nuts and tarragon, if used. Toss with dressing until greens are well coated.

Makes 4 servings.

FRESH FRUIT PLATTER

Preparation Time: 15 minutes
Cooking Time: None

1 melon (cantaloupe or honeydew)
2 red apples
1 can (8 ounces) pineapple
  chunks
1 pint fresh strawberries

½ cup pitted prunes
4 small Boston lettuces
1 pound cottage cheese
1 cup French dressing made
  with lemon juice
1 tablespoon honey

Wash all fruits that will be used unpeeled, and the lettuce, and drain well. On individual plates arrange the lettuce. Cut melon into 8 crosswise slices, scoop out seeds and peel each slice. Place melon ring on each plate; add cottage cheese in center; cube the remaining melon. Cut apples into eighths and remove cores. Dip apple slices into some of the dressing. Arrange apples, drained pineapple chunks, strawberries, prunes and melon cubes around the melon rings. Stir honey into the French dressing and serve with the salads.

Makes 4 large luncheon salads.

GREEN BEAN SALAD

Preparation Time: 5 minutes
Cooking Time: None

1 can (16 ounces) whole green
  beans, drained
¼ cup thinly sliced radishes
3 scallions, thinly sliced

½ cup French dressing
Salad greens
½ cup garlic croutons

In a medium-size bowl toss together beans, radishes, scallions, and dressing until vegetables are well coated. Arrange on salad greens and top with croutons.

Makes 4 servings.

HOT HAM AND POTATO SALAD

Preparation Time: 10 minutes
Cooking Time: 10 minutes

2 medium potatoes, peeled
  and diced
1 cup diced ham
1 small onion, finely chopped
2 ribs celery, slivered

¼ green pepper, finely
  chopped
1 tablespoon white vinegar
¼ cup mayonnaise
¼ cup sour cream

In a medium saucepan cook potato cubes in salted water until tender, about 10 minutes. Meanwhile, in a salad bowl combine ham, onion, celery and green pepper. Drain cooked potatoes and add vinegar, mayonnaise and sour cream. Pour over ham mixture and toss until well combined. Serve immediately.

Makes 2 main-dish servings.

MACARONI AND TUNA SALAD

Preparation Time: 4 minutes
Cooking Time: 10 minutes

1½ cups macaroni
1 can (6½ ounces) tuna fish,
  drained
2 tablespoons onion, finely
  chopped
2 tablespoons green pepper,
  finely chopped

1 carrot, grated
½ cup mayonnaise
1 tablespoon lemon juice
Salt, pepper
Salad greens

In a large saucepan cook macaroni in salted water until tender, about 10 minutes. Meanwhile, in a large bowl combine tuna, onion, green pepper, carrot, mayonnaise and lemon juice. Drain cooked macaroni in a colander and rinse with cold water until cool. Add to tuna mixture, season with salt and pepper and toss

until ingredients are well combined. Refrigerate until serving.
Serve on salad greens.

Makes 4 main-dish servings.

RAW MUSHROOM SALAD

Preparation Time: 12 minutes
Cooking Time: None

1 *pound medium mushrooms*
2 *scallions, finely chopped*
1 *teaspoon fresh parsley, finely chopped*

½ *cup French dressing made with lemon juice*
Salad greens (optional)

Wash and dry mushrooms; slice thinly into a medium-size bowl.
Add scallions, parsley and French dressing; toss until mushrooms are well coated. Arrange on salad greens or serve "as is"
for a summer vegetable.

Makes 4 to 6 servings.

RED-AND-WHITE SLAW

Preparation Time: 12 minutes
Cooking Time: None

1 *small head cabbage (about 1 pound)*
1 *small head red cabbage (about 1 pound)*
2 *tablespoons chopped scallions*
2 *tablespoons chopped green pepper*

½ *cup mayonnaise*
½ *cup sour cream*
1 *tablespoon cider vinegar*
1 *tablespoon sugar*
Salt and pepper

Wash and drain cabbage. Quickly shred with a very sharp
knife, one color at a time. Place shredded cabbage in two separate dishes. In a small bowl combine scallions, green pepper,

mayonnaise, sour cream, vinegar, sugar and salt and pepper to taste. Mix until well combined. Pour half the dressing over each kind of cabbage and toss separately until each is well coated with dressing. Arrange salad greens on a platter or in a large salad bowl. Mound red slaw in center and surround with the green slaw. Refrigerate until serving.
Makes 6 to 8 servings.

Variation: For a main-dish salad add a third ring of julienne strips of corned beef or ham.

SALAD NIÇOISE

Preparation Time: 8 minutes
Cooking Time: 10 minutes

2 *small potatoes, peeled and sliced*
1 *package (10 ounces) frozen small green beans*
Salad greens
1 *can (7 ounces) solid white tuna*
2 *hard-cooked eggs, quartered*
1 *small red onion, thinly sliced*
½ *green pepper, sliced into strips*

1 *can (2 ounces) anchovy fillets*
2 *tomatoes, cut into wedges*
¼ *cup black olives*
¼ *cup tarragon vinegar*
½ *cup salad oil*
1 *small clove garlic, pressed*
Salt and pepper

In large saucepan cook potatoes and green beans in salted water until just tender. Meanwhile arrange salad greens on a large platter. Place tuna in the center and arrange eggs, onion, green pepper, anchovy fillets, tomatoes and black olives around it, reserving several spaces for the potatoes and green beans. When potatoes and beans are tender, turn into a colander and rinse with cold water until they are cool. Combine vinegar, oil, garlic and salt and pepper to taste. Drizzle potatoes and beans with 3

tablespoons of this salad dressing and arrange them on the platter. Serve with remaining dressing.
Makes 4 main-dish servings.

SALAMAGUNDI SALAD

Preparation Time: 12 minutes
Cooking Time: None

1 *head romaine lettuce,
washed and broken into
pieces*
½ *cup cubed ham*
¼ *cup cubed Swiss cheese*
2 *tomatoes, cut in wedges*
1 *can (2 ounces) anchovy
fillets*

½ *cup black olives*
1 *can (2 ounces) pimiento,
cut into strips*
1 *cup garlic croutons*
2 *tablespoons wine vinegar*
¼ *cup salad oil*
Salt and pepper
¼ *cup mayonnaise*

Arrange lettuce in large salad bowl; top with rows of ham, cheese and tomatoes. Arrange anchovy fillets, black olives and pimiento between rows of ham, cheese, tomatoes. Top with croutons. Mix together wine vinegar, oil, salt, pepper and mayonnaise. Pour over salad and toss.
Makes 2 main-dish salads.

SPINACH SALAD

Preparation Time: 10 minutes
Cooking Time: None

½ *pound fresh spinach*
1 *small Bermuda onion, thinly
sliced*
½ *cup garbanzo (chick-peas)
or croutons*

1 *hard-cooked egg or ¼ cup
mayonnaise*
⅓ *cup French dressing*
Salt and pepper

Thoroughly wash spinach; dry on paper towels to absorb moisture. Remove stems and break in pieces into a medium-size salad bowl. Add onion, garbanzos or croutons, egg or mayonnaise, French dressing and salt and pepper to taste. Toss until ingredients are well coated with dressing.

Makes 4 servings.

VEGETABLE SALAD

Preparation Time: 10 minutes
Cooking Time: None

1 *head iceberg lettuce*
2 *tomatoes, cut into wedges*
¼ *cup sliced radishes*
½ *cucumber, thinly sliced*
½ *green pepper, cut into strips*
6 *medium mushrooms, thinly sliced*
4 *scallions, sliced*

1 *cup drained whole canned green beans*
½ *cup drained canned green peas*
¾ *cup French dressing*
crumbled blue cheese, optional
sour cream, optional

Wash and drain lettuce; break into pieces in a large salad bowl. Add remaining vegetables and French dressing and toss until well combined. Top with crumbled blue cheese combined with sour cream, if desired.

Makes 4 generous salads, 6 to 8 smaller salads.

WALDORF SALAD

Preparation Time: 12 minutes
Cooking Time: None

2 *cups cubed, unpeeled red apples*
½ *cup chopped celery*

¼ *cup coarsely chopped nuts*
½ *cup mayonnaise*
Salad greens

In a medium-size bowl toss together apples, celery, nuts and mayonnaise. Arrange on a bed of salad greens.

Makes 4 servings.

Note: For quick variations add sliced bananas, drained mandarin oranges or pineapple tidbits. For a main-dish variation add 1 cup cubed chicken or turkey.

WATERCRESS SALAD

Preparation Time: 5 minutes
Cooking Time: None

1 *bunch watercress*
Cherry tomatoes

French dressing
Freshly ground pepper

Wash watercress and trim tough ends. Heap portions on serving plates. Add tomatoes as garnish, top with French dressing, pepper.
Makes 2 servings.

Salad Dressings

BLENDER MAYONNAISE

Preparation Time: 4 minutes
Cooking Time: None

1 *egg (or 2 egg yolks)*
½ *teaspoon prepared mustard*
1 *teaspoon salt*

¼ *teaspoon sugar (optional)*
2 *tablespoons vinegar*
1 *cup salad oil*

Into container of blender put egg, mustard, salt, sugar, vinegar and ½ cup oil. Cover, blend 5 seconds until smooth. Without stopping motor, open lid and pour remaining oil into container in a steady stream. Blend only until oil is added and mixture is thick and smooth.
Makes 1¼ cups.

Note: If mayonnaise curdles, add 1 egg to the blender; slowly blend in the curdled mayonnaise.

BLUE CHEESE DRESSING

Preparation Time: 5 minutes
Cooking Time: None

4 *ounces* (1 *cup, crumbled*)   1 *tablespoon lemon juice*
   blue cheese   1 *small clove garlic, pressed*
1 *cup sour cream*   *Salt and pepper*

Mash blue cheese. Stir in remaining ingredients and season to taste. Refrigerate until serving.
   Makes about 2 cups.

CLASSIC FRENCH DRESSING

Preparation Time: 3 minutes
Cooking Time: None

¼ *cup cider or wine vinegar,*   ½ *teaspoon salt*
   or lemon juice   *Pepper*
¾ *cup olive oil or vegetable*   *Cayenne or dry mustard*
   oil

In a medium-size bottle mix all ingredients (pepper and cayenne or mustard to taste). Cover tightly and shake until combined.
   Makes about 1 cup.

GREEN GODDESS DRESSING

Preparation Time: 5 minutes
Cooking Time: None

½ *cup watercress leaves*   2 *tablespoons lemon juice*
3 *scallions, sliced*   2 *tablespoons salad oil*
3 *sprigs parsley*   ½ *teaspoon salt*
3 *anchovy fillets*   ¼ *teaspoon black pepper*
1 *cup mayonnaise*   ½ *cup sour cream*

Place all ingredients, except sour cream, into a blender; blend well. Turn into a serving dish and stir in sour cream. Refrigerate until serving.

Makes about 1¾ cups.

13 *Quick Breads and Believe-It-or-Not Cookies, Cakes, Pies*

This is a collection of breads you can bake in a blink, and cookies, small cakes and pastries to make a snack, to welcome guests or to round out a light meal.

The tradition of breads baked quickly goes back to the earliest cookery—when the griddle was the girdle of rocks around the campfire. Basic bread recipes are given here, from unleavened Indian pappadums, America's own hoecakes (sometimes cooked on a hoe placed over a fire) or johnnycakes. The name "johnny-cake" is said to be the "journey cake" baked by early American travelers to take with them on journeys.

For extra flavor, and extra nutrition, part whole-grain flours are used in some recipes. However, if you have none on hand, all-purpose flour may be used instead.

Cookies range from thin brownies to Proustian madeleines, to make new recollections of delicious nibbling.

Quickest Breads

BISCUITS

Preparation Time: 8 minutes
Baking Time: 12 minutes

2 cups all-purpose flour   ⅓ cup vegetable oil
3 teaspoons baking powder   ⅔ cup milk
1 teaspoon salt

Set oven to preheat to 425° F. Toss flour, baking powder and salt to mix. Combine oil and milk without stirring. Add all at once to flour and stir with a fork until mixture forms a ball and cleans the sides of the bowl. Knead about 10 times or until smooth. Roll or press out between sheets of waxed paper ¼ inch thick. Cut into diamonds or squares with a knife. Bake on ungreased cookie sheet in hot oven 10 to 12 minutes.
Makes 12 biscuits.

Variations: Add to flour mix ½ cup grated cheese; or ¼ cup crisp bacon crumbles or shredded ham; or 2 tablespoons finely chopped chives. Or make the biscuits sweet: Sprinkle with cinnamon and sugar before baking, or top with a bit of marmalade or jam.

BISCUITS—SOUR CREAM

Preparation Time: 16 minutes
Baking Time: 12 minutes

2 cups flour   ¾ cup sour cream
1 teaspoon baking soda   ¼ cup milk
1 teaspoon salt

Set oven to preheat to 475° F. Toss flour with soda and salt to mix. Add sour cream and milk to make a moist dough—a little more milk may be needed. Beat for a minute with a spoon, then roll out ¼ inch thick and cut into rounds; or shape into biscuits with the hands or a spoon. Bake in very hot oven, about 12 minutes, until browned and crisp.

Makes 12 biscuits.

CORN MUFFINS

Preparation Time: 13 minutes
Baking Time: 15 minutes

½ cup sifted flour
½ teaspoon baking soda
1¼ teaspoon baking powder
1 teaspoon salt
3 tablespoons sugar

1 cup cornmeal
1 egg, beaten
1¼ cups buttermilk
¼ cup butter, melted

Set oven to preheat to 450° F. Grease 1 dozen 2-inch muffin pans or cornstick molds. Toss flour with remaining dry ingredients to mix. Combine egg, buttermilk and melted butter; stir quickly into dry mixture. Fill pans ⅔ full. Bake in a hot oven 15 minutes. Serve hot with butter.

Makes 12 large muffins, 16 medium.

HOECAKE, OR JOHNNYCAKE

Preparation Time: 6 minutes
Baking Time: 12 minutes

½ teaspoon salt
1 cup cornmeal

1¼ cups boiling water
(about)

Add salt to cornmeal, pour boiling water over, and mix thoroughly to make a thick batter. Grease a 6-inch griddle (preferably black iron) with bacon fat or butter and spread out the batter into cakes about ½ inch thick or a little less. Cook on one side, put a dab of butter on top, turn to brown other side. Cook until golden brown and serve hot with butter and maple syrup or honey.

Makes 2 hoecakes.

IRISH BROWN BREAD ROLLS

Preparation Time: 12 minutes
Baking Time: 12 to 15 minutes

2 *cups whole-wheat flour and*   ¾ *teaspoon sugar*
    1 *cup white flour (or 3 cups*   1 *teaspoon baking soda*
    all-purpose flour)   1 *tablespoon butter*
¾ *teaspoon salt*   1 *cup buttermilk*

Set oven to preheat to 425° F. Combine the flours, salt, sugar and soda. Rub in the butter. Make a well in the center and gradually mix in the buttermilk. Stir with a wooden spoon, adding more liquid if necessary, to make a soft but manageable dough. With floured hands, knead the dough into a ball. Divide dough into 6 parts. Flatten each out in a circle about 1½ inches high. With a knife dipped in flour, make a cross in the center of each roll. Bake on greased cookie sheet in hot oven about 12 minutes, until browned and crisp. These keep well—taste better after a day.

Makes 6 rolls.

PAPPADUMS, OR "LAST MINUTE" BISCUITS

Preparation Time: 12 minutes
Cooking Time: 6 minutes

These are thin and blistered quick breads, generally served with curry, but a flavorful addition to any meal. And they're great at a campsite.

½ cup flour (½ of this whole wheat, if possible)
½ teaspoon salt
Dash of red pepper

3 tablespoons warm water or milk or cream (or just enough to make a thick paste)

Set oven to preheat to 425° F. or prepare oil for heating. Season flour, combine with liquid, knead very well, roll out a little, then cut into pieces of about 1 to 1½ inches in diameter. Take each piece and roll it and fold it and roll it again, finally beating it with the rolling pin against the table top, until it is paper thin, quite elastic, and about 3 to 6 inches in diameter. Prick each disk with tines of a fork. Drop into hot fat (360°) in a deep skillet; as soon as dough begins to puff, turn to brown lightly on other side, about ½ minute. Or place on a lightly greased and floured baking sheet and bake in a very hot oven for about 4 minutes, until browned and blistered. Because of size, bake in relays. Serve hot.

Makes 5 to 6 pappadums.

QUICK COFFEE MUFFINS

Preparation Time: 15 minutes
Baking Time: 15 minutes

CAKE

1 cup flour
½ cup sugar
1½ teaspoons baking powder
½ teaspoon salt
¼ cup shortening or ⅓ cup butter

1 egg
½ cup milk
1 teaspoon vanilla

TOPPING

⅓ cup brown or granulated sugar
1½ teaspoons cinnamon

⅓ cup chopped walnuts
2 tablespoons soft butter or margarine

Set oven to preheat to 375° F. Grease 12 muffin cups. Sift or toss flour, sugar, baking powder and salt to combine. Cut in shortening until flour is crumbly. Beat egg with milk and vanilla. Add to flour mixture and stir just until blended. Divide batter evenly among muffin cups. Combine ingredients for topping and sprinkle over surface, then pat down gently. Bake about 15 minutes, or until muffins are golden brown and tops spring back when touched. Serve warm.

Makes 12 muffins.

FRUITED COFFEE MUFFINS

Top each muffin with a teaspoon of cherry preserves before adding crumb topping, or place thin slices of apples, peaches or plums over batter, pressing down lightly. Then add topping and bake as above.

Baked and Top-of-Stove Treats

APPLE PANCAKE

Preparation Time: 6 minutes
Baking Time: 18 minutes

2 apples	*1 egg*
3 tablespoons butter	*¼ cup flour*
Cinnamon, nutmeg	*Pinch salt*
2 tablespoons sugar	*Cinnamon sugar*
¼ cup milk	

Preheat oven to 450° F. Peel and slice apples, cook in 2 tablespoons butter until tender, about 5 minutes. Meanwhile, with a rotary beater beat milk and egg, beat in flour and salt, and continue to beat until batter is very frothy. Melt 1 tablespoon butter in an ovenproof skillet. Add batter. Bake 12 minutes; prick bubbles on surface, spread with cooked apples. Sprinkle with spices and sugar. Set under broiler 5 minutes to glaze. Serve hot.

Makes 2 servings.

BRANDY SNAPS

Preparation Time: 7 minutes (for 2 batches)
Baking Time: 16 minutes

¼ cup (½ stick) butter
6 tablespoons sugar
2 tablespoons honey or light
  corn syrup

½ cup flour
1 teaspoon brandy

Set oven to preheat to 375° F. Cream butter with sugar, beat in honey with spoon. Stir in flour and brandy. Drop from teaspoon well apart on ungreased cookie sheet (lined with foil if desired). Bake about 8 minutes. Let cool 2 or 3 minutes, then remove. Repeat with remaining batter. If cookies become too brittle to remove, return to hot oven a minute or two.

Makes about 2 dozen.

BROWNIE THINS

Preparation Time: 15 minutes
Baking Time: 10 minutes

2 squares unsweetened chocolate
7 tablespoons butter (reserve 1
  tablespoon from ¼-pound
  stick)
¾ cup flour
½ teaspoon baking powder

½ teaspoon salt
1 cup sugar
2 eggs
1 teaspoon vanilla
½ cup broken walnut or pecan
  meats (buy chopped, or
  whirl in blender)

Place chocolate and butter in large bowl over hot water to melt. Set oven to preheat to 375° F. Grease 10 x 15-inch jelly-roll pan with reserved butter. Meanwhile, measure and combine flour, baking powder and salt, and toss to mix. Remove melted chocolate from heat, beat in sugar, then eggs. Stir in dry ingredients, then vanilla. Spread batter thinly in pan. Sprinkle top with chopped nuts. Bake 9 to 10 minutes, just until top springs back when touched. Cut immediately into bars or triangles. Remove from pan while warm.

Makes about 35 bars.

OATMEAL COOKIE BRITTLE

Preparation Time: 6 minutes
Baking Time: 20 minutes

½ cup butter
½ cup white sugar
½ cup brown sugar
1 egg
2½ cups oats
½ teaspoon baking soda

½ teaspoon salt
½ cup chopped nuts
½ cup raisins
½ cup semisweet chocolate
  pieces
½ teaspoon vanilla

Set oven to preheat to 375° F. Cream butter and sugars. Add egg, beat well. Add remaining ingredients and blend thoroughly. Drop from a teaspoon, 1 inch apart, on a greased cookie sheet. Bake about 10 minutes. Let stand on cookie sheet 1 minute before removing.

Makes about 4 dozen cookies.

Note: If desired, bake half of the cookies. Place remainder on foil or other rack, form into bar, refrigerate, and slice to bake as needed.

DROP DOUGHNUTS 'LASSES

Preparation Time: 7 minutes
Frying Time: 16 minutes

1¼ cups flour
1½ teaspoons baking powder
½ teaspoon salt
½ teaspoon cinnamon
1 tablespoon oil
½ cup molasses (or sugar)

1 egg
¼ cup milk
¼ cup orange juice
Oil for frying (to depth of 2 inches)

Combine dry ingredients. Add remaining ingredients and stir to blend. Dip teaspoon into hot fat, fill with dough, drop 4 to 6 doughnuts at a time into fat in deep pan. Fry each batch about 5 minutes until doughnuts are golden and have risen to surface, turning to brown both sides. Drain on paper towels. Continue until all the dough is used. Sprinkle with confectioners' sugar.

Makes about 18 doughnuts.

JELLY ROLL

Preparation Time: 15 minutes
Baking Time: 10 minutes

2 tablespoons butter
3 eggs
¾ cup sugar

1 teaspoon vanilla
⅔ cup pancake mix

Preheat oven to 400° F. Grease a 10- x 15-inch jelly-roll pan, line with waxed paper, sprinkle with flour. Melt butter. Beat eggs until foamy, gradually beating in ¾ cup sugar. Stir in butter, vanilla, and pancake mix. Pour batter into prepared pan. Bake 10 minutes. Turn out on towel sprinkled with confectioners' sugar. Carefully remove paper. Spread with raspberry, strawberry or other jelly, roll up.

CHOCOLATE CREAM ROLL

Preparation Time: 20 minutes
Baking Time: 10 minutes

Make cake for Jelly Roll (page 191). Roll up in towel, cool in refrigerator 5 minutes. Meanwhile, whip 1 cup heavy cream stiff with 2 tablespoons instant cocoa mix. Unroll cake, spread with cream filling, roll up again and serve.

LADYFINGERS

Preparation Time: 10 minutes
Baking Time: 15 minutes

½ cup plus 1 tablespoon
  granulated sugar
3 eggs, separated
1 teaspoon vanilla

⅔ cup sifted flour
Pinch salt
¼ cup sifted confectioners'
  sugar

Combine ½ cup granulated sugar, egg yolks and vanilla in mixing bowl. Beat until mixture is thick and pale yellow. Fold in flour to make a firm batter. Beat egg whites with salt until soft peaks form. Gradually add sugar and continue to beat until peaks are stiff. Fold egg whites into cake batter. Fill 3¾-inch ladyfinger molds with batter, or pipe out on cookie sheets, and sprinkle with confectioners' sugar. Bake in moderately slow oven (300° F.) for 12 to 15 minutes or until pale brown.
  Makes about 40.

MADELEINES

Preparation Time: 10 minutes
Baking Time: 15 minutes

1 cup confectioners' sugar
2 cups sifted cake flour
4 eggs

Pinch of salt
1 teaspoon vanilla
1 cup melted butter

Combine sugar, flour, eggs, salt and vanilla in a bowl. Work with a spatula until the mixture is smooth. Work in the melted butter. Butter thoroughly trays of 12 hollow, shell-shaped, 3-inch madeleine molds or cupcake pans and fill ⅔ full. Bake in a moderately hot (375° F.) oven for 15 minutes, or until golden brown.

Makes 3 dozen.

Note: This recipe traditionally calls for melted and clarified butter—that is, skimmed of foam and solids. In the interest of time, I tested this recipe both with clarified butter (which generally makes for a smoother, softer texture) and as above. No perceptible difference, so save the 5 minutes!

MERINGUE BARS

Preparation Time: 10 minutes
Baking Time: 18 minutes

½ *cup* (1 *stick*) *butter*
½ *cup sugar*
1 *egg yolk*
1 *cup flour*
1 *egg white*

¼ *cup finely chopped,*
blanched almonds
2 *tablespoons sugar*
¼ *teaspoon cinnamon*

Set oven to preheat to 400° F. Grease a 9- x 13-inch pan. Cream butter and sugar until light. Beat in egg yolk. Cut in flour. Spread dough thinly in pan. Beat egg white stiff. Spread on top of dough. Combine nuts, sugar and cinnamon and sprinkle over top. Bake until golden and edges shrink slightly from side of pan, about 20 minutes. While warm, cut into bars 1¾ by 3 inches.

Makes 24 bars.

PANCAKE CAKE

Preparation Time: 3 minutes
Cooking Time: 12 minutes

Prepare batter for pancakes as directed on the package. In a 10-inch skillet, make double-sized pancakes, using about ½ cup batter for each cake. Keep pancakes warm in the oven until all batter is used. Shape a "layer cake" by stacking 3 or 4 cakes with a filling of apple sauce, apple butter, or fruit jam between layers; sprinkle top with brown sugar or with a combination of cinnamon and white sugar. Serve piping hot.

SCONES

Preparation Time: 12 minutes
Baking Time: 12 minutes

1 *cup flour*	2 *tablespoons butter*
1 *teaspoon baking powder*	1 *egg, beaten*
¼ *teaspoon salt*	¼ *cup light cream or milk*
1 *teaspoon brown sugar*	2 *tablespoons raisins*

Set oven to preheat to 450° F. or heat heavy griddle. Toss flour, baking powder, salt and sugar to combine. Blend in butter. Beat egg; add to flour mixture with cream or milk. Add raisins. Beat with spoon for 1 minute. Turn out on floured board, roll out ½ inch thick, and quickly cut into rounds or squares. Place on cookie sheet or griddle. Bake 12 minutes in oven or about 6 minutes each side on griddle.

Makes 6 scones.

STRAWBERRY SHORTCAKE

Preparation Time: 15 minutes
Baking Time: 12 minutes

*Strawberries, sliced and sweet-
ened to taste*

Heavy cream
Biscuits (page 184)

Bake biscuits, adding 1 tablespoon sugar to the ingredients and substituting cream for the milk. Bake as directed. Meanwhile, prepare berries and whip cream. Butter hot biscuits, layer with sweetened sliced berries, top with more berries and with whipped cream.

Variations: Layer shortcake with fresh or canned peaches and /or other fruits.
Use waffles (below) in place of biscuits.

WAFFLES

Preparation Time: 17 minutes
Baking Time: 12 minutes

⅓ cup butter
2 cups flour
2 teaspoons baking powder
1 teaspoon salt

1 tablespoon sugar
3 eggs, separated
1½ cups milk

Melt butter. Toss dry ingredients to blend. Beat egg whites stiff. With same beater, beat egg yolks, milk and melted butter together. Combine with dry ingredients. Mix until well blended, and fold in stiffly beaten egg whites. Bake on a hot waffle iron.
Makes 8 large waffles.

Variations: Add ¾ cup chopped nuts, pitted prunes, dates, raisins or a mixture of any or all of these to batter; or sprinkle batter for each waffle with 2 tablespoons blueberries. Bake on a hot waffle iron.

WAFFLE SUNDAES

Top hot baked waffles with ice cream, any sweetened fruit and whipped cream. Serve at once.

Also see Pies or Tarts, page 218.

14 *Divine Desserts*

The most beautiful of all desserts may be a simple tribute to the day, the meal and the mood—and take next to no time to prepare. Arrange fresh washed whole berries on a plate, stems intact, with sugar or yogurt for dipping. Serve up a chilled orange, perfectly peeled, or an apple and a wedge of ripe Camembert or Brie cheese, kept at room temperature while dinner is served, or make coffee into a sipping Irish or international dessert, or pass a bowl of nuts and a bottle of Madeira or tiny glasses of liqueur.

Then again, you might want another kind of dessert, a cool and frothy finale for a hearty meal, or a warm and satisfying dessert to round out a light meal. Here are the how-to's, from fruit gelatin to a quick mousse that sets in minutes instead of hours, and from Chocolate Mousse for Two to Chocolate Fondue for a crowd. Add ice-cream specialties from Peach Melba to Pear Hélène—or bake an Alaska for a party.

Whether you choose a quick-sliced Ambrosia or go the whole way with Zabaglione, dessert marks the finale of a meal planned for pleasure, your own as well as guests'.

AMBROSIA

Preparation Time: 8 minutes
Cooking Time: None

2 *large navel oranges*   ⅔ *cup shredded coconut*
2 *tablespoons confectioners'*
  sugar (*optional*)

Peel oranges, removing white inner skin and catching any juice in a bowl. Cut fruit into thin slices, crosswise. Arrange slices on platter or individual serving plates. Sprinkle with sugar if desired and pour any reserved juice over. Top with shredded coconut. Chill until serving.
Makes 2 to 4 servings.

Apples and . . .

Preparation Time: 3 minutes
Cooking Time: None

A bowl of chilled apples, tart and winey, so that when you bite into a wedge the juice bursts into cider in your mouth, with a wedge of cheese softened to room temperature, or a few walnuts to crack as you munch, sherry to sip, or smooth chocolate to set off the fruit . . . any of these are quick dessert bliss. For perfection, choose your apples according to season.

Early Summer:
Granny Smiths, if you can find them—and don't let the green skin fool you. The meat is white, juicy and fresh-flavored. Imports reach here before our own apples ripen, from New Zealand orchards, where seasons reverse ours.

Late Summer, Early Fall:
McIntosh and other thin-skinned early apples. These are

juicy to eat out of hand, make delectable quick apple sauce; at their best when fresh, though now available the year round.

Autumn and Winter:
Delicious apples, bright red or golden, Jonathans, Winesaps. Rich apples, hearty in flavor and bite. Look for firm skins, a closed star-shaped blossom at the narrow end. Smaller apples, with deeper "points," are often more flavorful than the largest, most symmetrical fruits.

APPLE CRISP QUICKIE

Preparation Time: 12 minutes
Cooking Time: 15 minutes

4 *apples, green or red*
2 *tablespoons butter*
2 *tablespoons raisins*
½ *cup brown sugar*
¾ *cup flour (or ½ part oatmeal)*

½ *teaspoon cinnamon*
½ *teaspoon nutmeg*
⅓ *cup butter*

Set oven to preheat to 450° F. Peel and slice apples. Heat butter in oven-proof skillet, add apples and raisins. Cook, turning occasionally, about 2 minutes, until apples become glazed. Meanwhile, blend remaining ingredients, using fork or fingers, to make a crumbly mixture. Sprinkle crumbs over apples, then pat down to cover evenly. Bake about 15 minutes, until crumbs are crisped and brown.
    Makes 4 to 6 servings.

APPLE RINGS WITH CINNAMON

Preparation Time: 6 minutes
Cooking Time: 12 minutes

1 *cup water*
¾ *cup sugar*
1 *piece stick cinnamon, ¾
    inch long*

2 *red apples*

Bring water and sugar to boil in a skillet, stirring until sugar dissolves. Add cinnamon stick; simmer 3 minutes. Meanwhile, core apples and slice into rings, ¾ inch thick. Poach slices in the syrup, turning once, until the fruit is translucent. Remove fruit with slotted spatula to serving platter, letting syrup boil down until thickened. Pour syrup over apple slices. Serve warm or cold.

Makes 2 to 4 servings.

APPLE SAUCE, UNCOOKED

Preparation Time: 5 minutes
Cooking Time: None

2 *large apples*
1 *cup cold water*
1½ *tablespoons lemon juice*

1 *tablespoon confectioners'
    sugar, to taste*

Cut apples in half; remove cores but do not peel. Then cut into cubes. Drop cubes into bowl of water with lemon juice. Place ¼ cup of liquid in blender container, add ½ cup apples at a time. Cover, blend about 5 seconds, until smooth. Remove to bowl and repeat with remaining apples, scraping down sides as necessary. Serve promptly.

Makes 2 servings.

Berry Variation: In place of sugar, blend 2 tablespoons berry preserves with apples.

Raisin Apple Sauce Variation: Stir ¼ cup raisins and ¼ teaspoon cinnamon into blended apples.

Also see Shortcuts: Apple Sauce (page 29).

APPLE WHIP

Preparation Time: 6 to 11 minutes
Chilling Time: 10 minutes

½ cup heavy cream, very cold   1 cup Apple Sauce, Uncooked
2 tablespoons powdered sugar   (page 200), or canned
1 teaspoon vanilla

Whip cream until thick, add sugar and vanilla, whip until stiff. Fold into apple sauce. Heap into individual serving dishes and place in freezer or refrigerator 10 minutes to chill.
   Makes 2 to 4 servings.

   Note: You could use 1 cup prepared whipped topping in place of cream, sugar and vanilla above. The volume is the same, flavor is your choice. I prefer the fresh cream and consider the result well worth 4 minutes of whipping. Dieters may want to use Low Calorie Whip (page 224).

APRICOT WHIP

Preparation Time: 4 minutes
Cooking Time: None

1 cup apricot halves, canned   1 cup heavy cream
   or stewed dried   1 tablespoon confectioners'
¼ cup apricot juice from can   sugar
   or stewing liquid   ⅛ teaspoon almond extract

Place apricots in blender container with liquid. Blend smooth, stopping and pushing apricots down from sides with spatula if necessary. Remove apricots to bowl. Add to same container (no need to wash) cream, sugar and almond extract. Whip cream, flicking switch on and off or using spurt set, about 10 seconds or until thick. Add to pureed apricots and fold in. Chill until serving time.

Makes 4 servings.

APRICOT YOGURT WHIP

Prepare apricots in blender as above. Add 1 cup plain yogurt, 1 tablespoon honey, and mix together. Chill until ready to serve.

BAKED ALASKA

Preparation Time: 10 minutes
Baking Time: 5 minutes

1 *loaf sponge cake or pound cake*
1 *or 2 pints ice cream, frozen hard*
4 *egg whites*

½ *teaspoon salt*
1 *tablespoon lemon juice or vinegar*
½ *cup sugar*

Buy cake and defrost if frozen. Cut the base off lengthwise in a strip 1 inch high and ¼ inch larger on all sides than a pint brick of ice cream. Place the cake on a sheet of foil or heavy paper on a baking sheet. Set oven to preheat to 450° F. Break 4 egg whites into a bowl, add salt and whip until whites are foamy. Add lemon juice or vinegar and 2 tablespoons of sugar at a time, beating after each addition, until whites stand in *very stiff* peaks when beater is lifted. Remove ice cream from carton, and center on top of cake strip, placing bricks of ice cream one on the other, if two are used. Frost quickly with meringue, covering ice cream completely and coming down over sides of cake. Swirl top with spatula. Bake in hot oven about 5 minutes, just until lightly browned. Slip onto platter and serve at once. Reserve rest of sponge cake for other uses.

Makes 6 to 10 servings.

BANANAS AND TOPPING

Preparation Time: 3 minutes
Cooking Time: None

2 *small bananas or* 1 *large*   Brown *sugar, or* walnuts in
¼ *cup sour cream or yogurt*   *syrup or honey* (*optional*)

Peel bananas and slice into serving dishes. Top with sour cream
or yogurt. Sprinkle with brown sugar or walnuts in syrup or
honey. Serve immediately.
    Makes 2 servings.

    Note: This is a dessert you can put together after the main
course is finished, while the coffee or tea brews. Keep bananas in
a decorative fruit bowl to ripen—a double-duty centerpiece and
dessert.

BANANAS FLAMBEES

Preparation Time: 3 minutes
Cooking Time: 9 minutes

2 *tablespoons butter*   2 *tablespoons brown sugar*
2 *to* 4 *firm, ripe bananas* (*yel-* ¼ *cup rum or brandy or*
    low or red)   *orange liqueur*

Melt butter in a serving skillet (copper is ideal). Meanwhile,
peel and cut bananas in half lengthwise. Add to skillet. Brown
cut side first, turn and brown second side. Sprinkle with brown
sugar, baste with butter in pan and spoon sauce over, cooking
a minute or two to glaze. Add liquor to pan, heat a few seconds,
and tilt to flame to ignite. As soon as flames burst up, remove
pan from heat. Spoon sauce over bananas and serve.
    Makes 2 to 4 servings.

BERRY BASKET CAKE

Preparation Time: 18 minutes
Cooking Time: None

1 *pint blueberries, fresh or un-sweetened frozen*
½ *pint raspberries or straw-berries or 1 cup sliced peaches*

2 *sponge-cake layers, about 8 inches in diameter*
2 *cups whipped cream*
⅓ *cup red jelly, melted with 1 tablespoon apricot liqueur*

Wash berries and remove stems if necessary. Place one cake layer on serving plate. Spread with ⅓ of whipped cream. Top with ⅓ of berries, and spoon ⅓ of jelly glaze over. Place second layer of cake over and press down slightly. Spread with remaining berries and coat with remainder of whipped cream. Finish with jelly glaze. Chill until serving time.

Makes 10 servings.

BERRY BONUS—BLUEBERRIES & CO.

Preparation Time: 3 minutes
Cooking Time: None

Wash blueberries and remove any stems just before serving, in your choice of 6 berry-good ways:

Berries plain—a satisfying, low-calorie dessert.

Berries and cream—a classic, delectable with sweet cream or sour, or with whipped cream, or with low-calorie whipped topping.

Berries and ice cream—or sherbet.

Berries in wine or champagne—worth a toast.

Berries and fruit liqueur—great after-dinner combo.

Berries and other fruit—especially great with sliced banana, other berry varieties, peaches, watermelon balls or cantaloupe.

Allow ½ cup of berries per serving, which is 1 fruit portion on most low-calorie diet plans. Count on 4 servings per pint of berries.

BERRY TARTS

Preparation Time: 9 minutes
Cooking Time: None

½ pint berries—blueberries,
raspberries or strawberries
3 ounces cream cheese
2 tablespoons milk or light
cream
1 tablespoon confectioners'
sugar or honey

½ teaspoon vanilla
4 tart shells
4 tablespoons fruit liqueur
(optional)

Wash and stem berries if necessary. Beat cream cheese with milk and sugar or honey and vanilla. Put 2 tablespoons of cheese mixture into each tart shell. Heap berries into shell. Spoon 1 tablespoon liqueur over each, if desired, to flavor and glaze.
Makes 4 servings.

CANTALOUPE VARIATIONS

Preparation Time: 4 minutes
Cooking Time: None

Cut a small ripe cantaloupe in half, scoop out seeds and serve with a wedge of lemon or lime, or sweetened lime juice, or salt, to accent sweet flavor. Or try these variations:

Melon au Porto: Fill hollow of prepared melon with port wine.

Cooler: Fill hollow of prepared melon with sherbet.

Creamy: Fill hollow of prepared melon with ice cream—especially peach.

Berry Basket: Fill hollow of prepared melon with berries.

Dieter: Fill hollow of prepared melon with cottage cheese, or better yet, serve plain.

CHERRIES JUBILEE

Preparation Time: 3 minutes
Cooking Time: 10 to 12 minutes

1 can (1 *pound or more*) *Bing*
 cherries
½ *teaspoon cinnamon*

¼ to ½ *cup brandy or Cognac*
1 *quart vanilla ice cream*

Pour juice from cherries into chafing pan or into a fondue pot. Heat to boiling and boil rapidly for 5 minutes to reduce liquid. Stir in cinnamon. Add cherries; heat. Heat brandy or Cognac in a ladle or warming pan. Ignite; spoon flaming sauce over cherries and serve, still flaming, over vanilla or other ice cream.
 Makes 6 to 8 servings.

CHINESE FRUIT DISH

Preparation Time: 5 minutes
Cooking Time: None

1 *can* (8 *to* 12 *ounces*) *lychees*
1 *can* (8 *to* 12 *ounces*)
 mandarin orange sections

Chill both cans. Open. Drain fruits and arrange in a bowl with picks for self help.

Makes 4 to 6 servings.

CHOCOLATE FONDUE

Preparation Time: 5 minutes
Cooking Time: 4 minutes

6 *ounces semisweet chocolate pieces or sweet chocolate, broken up*
⅓ *cup sour cream*
2 *tablespoons kirsch, or mint liqueur or coffee liqueur*

Strawberries
Pineapple or apple wedges
Cake cubes

Heat chocolate with sour cream, stirring constantly, until smooth. Stir in liqueur and hold over warmer on serving tray. Add a little more liqueur if mixture becomes too thick. Arrange fruits, cake cubes and long-handled fondue forks on tray. Guests spear fruit or cake on forks, twirl in chocolate—blissful dessert.

Makes 4 to 6 servings.

CHOCOLATE MOUSSE FOR TWO

Preparation Time: 20 minutes
Cooking Time: 5 minutes

2 *ounces semisweet chocolate (or chocolate bar)*
2 *eggs, separated*
Pinch salt

1 *tablespoon confectioners' sugar*
2 *tablespoons soft butter*
1 *tablespoon brandy*

Melt chocolate over very low heat. Remove from heat; cool by setting pan over ice cubes. Meanwhile, separate eggs. Beat whites with pinch of salt until soft peaks form. Add sugar; beat until very stiff peaks hold when beater is removed. Beat egg yolks until thick and light. Add cooled chocolate slowly, beating until well blended. Beat in butter, a tablespoon at a time. Add brandy and stir smooth. Fold in egg whites. Place in freezer for 10 to 15 minutes.

Makes 2 servings.

COCOA FLUFF CHARLOTTE

Preparation Time: 8 minutes
Cooking Time: None

2 tablespoons Cognac
2 tablespoons water
24 ladyfingers
1½ cups heavy sweet cream

⅓ cup confectioners' sugar
3 tablespoons cocoa
Dash salt

Combine Cognac and water. Dip ladyfingers quickly in and out of liquor mixture, then lay out in a row on a flat platter. Place cream, sugar, cocoa and salt in bowl or container of electric blender. Beat or blend, stirring down with rubber spatula if necessary, until mixture is smooth and thick, about 45 seconds. Heap moistened ladyfingers with cocoa fluff.

Makes 8 servings.

COEUR A LA CREME

Preparation Time: 6 minutes
Cooking Time: None

⅓ cup cream, sweet or sour
½ cup cottage cheese
1 package (3 ounces) cream cheese
¼ cup sugar

1 teaspoon vanilla
Fresh strawberries or 1 package (10 ounces) frozen strawberries, slightly thawed

Whip or blend cream with cheeses, sugar and vanilla until very smooth. Form into heart shape on chilled serving plate (or turn into heart-shaped mold lined with cheesecloth, then out on plate). Surround with whole fresh berries or frozen berries.

Makes 4 servings.

Coffees International

Preparation Time: 3 minutes
Cooking Time: 6 minutes

Coffee is dessert, too, when you spike it with liquor, top with whipped cream and serve in a warmed goblet. Here's dessert drama, surefire appeal, with on-the-spot preparation. Brew coffee dark and strong. The better the coffee, the better the drink.

IRISH COFFEE

Pour 1 jigger Irish whiskey into warmed goblet. Add a cube of sugar if you like. Tilt to flame and ignite if you like—dramatic, and this burns off the alcohol, leaves flavor. Fill with hot coffee, top with unsweetened whipped cream. That's all.

FRENCH COFFEE

Prepare as above, with Cointreau or brandy instead of whiskey.

ITALIAN COFFEE

Prepare as above, with anisette instead of whiskey.

COMPOTE

Preparation Time: 1 minute
Cooking Time: 5–6 minutes

Bring dried pitted prunes, apricot halves, golden raisins, sliced apple and a lemon or orange slice, to boil with water to cover. Boil covered, 5 to 6 minutes. Remove from heat. Add port or sherry to replace absorbed water. Serve warm or chilled.

Variation: Add dried figs cut in half, and honey or sugar if desired.

CREPES COINTREAU

Preparation Time: 5 minutes
Cooking Time: 12 minutes

1 recipe Crêpes (page 131)
4 tablespoons butter
1 large orange

6 large sugar cubes
4 ounces Cointreau

Prepare crêpes, using cream and additional egg yolks. Fold cooked crêpes in quarters. Heat 4 tablespoons butter in pan. Rub orange rind with 6 sugar cubes, drop sugar into pan. Cut orange and squeeze juice into pan. Cook until caramelized. Add 2 jiggers (3 ounces) Cointreau and cook until smooth, stirring constantly. Add crêpes and heat, spooning sauce over. Add remainder of Cointreau (or brandy) if desired, tilt to flame to ignite, or heat liqueur in ladle, then ignite and pour over. Remove from heat and serve when flames die down.

FRUIT FRITTERS

Preparation Time: 8 minutes
Cooking Time: 10 minutes

Oil for frying
2 apples cored and cut into slices, or 2 bananas peeled and cut into chunks

1 cup prepared pancake mix with 1 extra egg added
confectioners' sugar

Heat oil in deep pan; oil should be 2 inches deep. Prepare fruit and batter. Dip each piece of fruit into batter and fry, a few at a time, until crisp and golden. Drain on paper towels. Dust with confectioners' sugar. Serve hot.

Makes 2 to 4 servings for dessert or snacks.

FRUITED GELATIN

Preparation Time: 5 minutes
Chilling Time: 15 minutes

1 package (3 ounces) fruit-flavored gelatin
1 cup hot water

1 cup ice cubes
1 banana, mashed, or other fruit, diced

Prepare gelatin as directed, using 1 cup hot water to dissolve. Then add ice cubes and stir until melted and gelatin begins to thicken. Beat in mashed banana, or stir in other diced fruit. Pour into serving dishes. Set in freezer for 15 minutes.

Makes 4 servings.

FRUITED RICOTTA CHEESE

Preparation Time: 8 minutes
Cooking Time: None

¼ *cup glazed or dried fruits*
   cut up
2 *tablespoons raisins*
1 *tablespoon rum or liqueur*

½ *pound ricotta cheese*
½ *square (½ ounce) semi-*
   sweet chocolate, grated

Combine fruit and raisins, soaked with rum, with ricotta cheese. Divide mixture among 8 dessert dishes. Sprinkle each portion with grated chocolate.
   Makes 4 servings.

   Variation: Spoon ricotta into dessert dishes and serve choice of fruit separately; or sprinkle with brown sugar.

GREEN GRAPES, SOUR CREAM AND BROWN SUGAR

Preparation Time: 5 minutes
Cooking Time: None

Green grapes, seedless
Sour cream

Brown sugar

Wash and stem chilled grapes. Place in serving dish. Top with flat layer of sour cream to cover surface. Sprinkle with brown sugar. Chill until serving time.

GUAVA AND CHEESE

Preparation Time: 2 minutes
Cooking Time: None

Canned guava shells
Cream cheese or fresh semisoft
   cheese

Buy canned guava shells in Spanish section of supermarket or in gourmet shop. Serve 1 shell with wedge of cream cheese or fresh semisoft cheese (mozzarella or other) for each portion.

ICE CREAM DESSERTS

A half-hour cook's standby dessert. Simply scoop and top with liqueur, fruits or grated chocolate. Pile ice cream on a split banana, top with chocolate syrup or your choice of dessert sauces (page 225) or make a Baked Alaska (page 202), Parfait (page 218), Peach Melba (page 216), Pear Hélène (page 221) or top with Cherries Jubilee (page 206). Put a scoop into a tall glass, fill with *hot* coffee for a combination dessert and drink that's the best of hot and cold!

MANGO

Preparation Time: 3 minutes
Cooking Time: None

Mangos generally arrive in markets green and unripe and, like bananas, ripen well at room temperature—another centerpiece fruit. This flattish, pear-curved fruit is unusually sweet and juicy when ripe, and the sweetest meat is closest to the large seed to which it clings. Just peel with a very sharp knife or cut into sections and serve on the shell with a spoon, offering the seed to an *aficionado* for tasty nibbling. Cubed mango also adds delectable flavor to a fruit cup. When ripe, mango is soft to the touch, and the skin may become mottled with black spots.

MOCHA SOUFFLE

Preparation Time: 15 minutes
Baking Time: 15 minutes

3 tablespoons butter
3 tablespoons flour
2 tablespoons cocoa
¾ cup strong coffee
¼ cup cream

½ cup sugar
¼ teaspoon salt
½ teaspoon vanilla
4 eggs, separated
¼ teaspoon cream of tartar

Preheat oven to 425° while you prepare the soufflé. Melt butter, stir in flour and cocoa to combine. Gradually add coffee and cream and cook over low heat, stirring until the mixture is smooth and thick. Add sugar, salt and vanilla, stirring until smooth. Beat egg whites stiff with cream of tartar; with same beater beat yolks until light. Combine egg yolks thoroughly with coffee mixture. Fold in ¼ the egg whites with an over-and-over motion, gently but very thoroughly. Fold in the remaining egg whites carefully and lightly. Have ready 4 individual soufflé dishes, about 1½-cup capacity, buttered and sprinkled with sugar. Divide batter among dishes. Bake in hot oven (425° F.) about 15 minutes, until puffed and browned. Serve at once.

Makes 4 servings.

MOUSSE COOLER

Preparation Time: 3 minutes
Chilling Time: 6 minutes

½ cup boiling water
1 package (3 ounces) fruit-
   flavored gelatin

½ cup any fruit, except fresh
   pineapple, coarsely cut
1½ cups crushed ice or 1 pint
   ice cream

Put boiling water and gelatin into container of electric blender. Cover and blend 5 seconds, until gelatin is dissolved. Add fruit and crushed ice or ice cream in pieces. Blend 20 seconds, until smooth. Pour into individual dishes. Chill 6 minutes.

Makes 4 servings.

NUTS AND WINE

Preparation Time: 2 minutes
Cooking Time: None

Walnuts or pecans or mixed nuts   *Port or sherry or Madeira*

Pile nuts into a bowl. Pass with nutcracker. Serve with wine in your most graceful glasses.

Variation: Add a bowl of raisins or apples for pleasant flavor contrast. Great for a winter evening.

ORANGE CLASSIC

Preparation Time: 8 minutes
Cooking Time: 5 minutes

4 navel oranges
½ cup sugar   *½ cup water (or part white wine)*

Peel oranges with very sharp knife, discarding inner white pith. Reserve some of the outer peel, cut into slivers. Cut oranges into slices ½ inch thick. Reassemble, using picks to secure. Combine sugar, water, wine and orange-peel slivers in skillet. Boil to dissolve sugar and thicken slightly. Pour over fruit. Serve warm or chilled.

Makes 4 servings.

Note: Keep oranges in the refrigerator for chilled dessert ready as is. The same applies to tangerines or tangelos, available in winter.

PEACH MELBA

Preparation Time: 5 minutes
Cooking Time: None

2 *large peach halves, fresh*   2 *scoops ice cream*
   peeled or canned   4 *tablespoons raspberry sauce*

Place each peach half in a serving dish. Top with scoop of ice cream and 2 tablespoons Berry Sauce—recipe page 225 or from a jar or made by thinning raspberry preserves with a little orange liqueur or water.

PEACHES—FRESH

Preparation Time: 1 minute
Cooking Time: None

A bowl of fresh peaches makes a delicious dessert to eat either out of hand or French style, with a fork and knife for peeling, a shaker of confectioners' sugar to sprinkle to taste. That's just the beginning.

PEACHES—QUICK SLICED

Preparation Time: 5 minutes
Cooking Time: None

Wash, dry and cut 2 peaches into thin wedges, discarding pits. Toss slices with 1 tablespoon glucose or confectioners' sugar and the juice of 1 orange.

Makes 2 servings or 4 servings with ice cream or whipped cream.

PEACHES—STEWED

Preparation Time: 6 minutes
Cooking Time: 11 minutes

1 *pound ripe peaches*
Water

½ *cup sugar* (*or to taste*)
½ *lemon*

Place peaches in pan with boiling water to cover. Boil 5 minutes. Remove peaches and plunge into cold water. Reserve 1½ cups of the cooking liquid in pan. Add sugar and bring to a boil. Add juice of lemon. Slip skins from peaches, cut into halves or wedges, free from the seeds and drop into pan with water. Add a few peach seeds to the water for extra flavor. Stew 4 to 6 minutes. Strain syrup and pour over peaches. Serve warm or chilled.

Makes 4 servings.

PEACHES IN WINE

Use 1 cup red wine in place of 1 cup of cooking liquid in second stage. Add ¼ teaspoon cinnamon before cooking.

PEAR PLUS

Preparation Time: 2 minutes
Cooking Time: None

Serve a very ripe pear (Bartlett is especially good) with a wedge of Bel Paese cheese—a natural, superlative affinity.

RUM-CHOCOLATE PARFAIT

Preparation Time: 12 minutes
Cooking Time: None

1 *cup chocolate-chip cookie crumbs*	2 *tablespoons rum* 1 *pint ice cream*

Roll or blend cookies to make crumbs. Add rum to crumbs. Spoon ice cream into the bottom of each of 4 tall slender parfait glasses. Top with spoonful of cookie-crumb mix. Continue until you have made 3 layers of ice cream, each topped with cookie-crumb mix.

Makes 4 servings.

Variations: Alternate ice cream layers with preserves or berries or fruits or liqueur.

Tip: Prepare parfaits; store in freezer until serving time.

10-Minute Pies or Tarts

CRUMB CRUST

Preparation Time: 10 minutes
Cooking Time: None

18 *graham crackers* (1½ *cups crumbs*)	¼ *cup melted butter* ¼ *cup sugar*

Crush crackers with a rolling pin to make fine crumbs, or grind in the blender. Add butter and sugar, combining well. Press against bottom and sides of a buttered 8- or 9-inch pie plate. Chill the crust for 5 minutes or longer. Fill as below. Vanilla, chocolate or ginger wafers may be substituted for the graham crackers.

FRESH FRUIT PIE

Spread the prepared crumb crust with stemmed and washed berries, or sliced ripe peaches, pears or bananas. Melt ½ cup of clear, bright-colored jelly over low heat. Pour this glaze over the fruit and serve at once.

FRUIT CREAM PIE

Prepare a package of instant vanilla pudding made with 1 cup milk, 1 cup sour cream. Fill crumb crust and chill until serving time. Garnish with cherries, strawberries, bananas, pineapple or other choice of fruit.

SWEET PASTRY SHELL

Preparation Time: 12 minutes
Baking Time: 12 minutes

1½ cups flour
7 tablespoons butter or margarine
¼ cup sugar
1 egg

2 tablespoons sour cream or 1 tablespoon lemon juice and 1 additional tablespoon butter or margarine

Set oven to preheat to 425° F. Spoon flour into wide bowl or onto pastry board. Make well in center. Drop remaining ingredients in center. Mix butter, sugar, egg, cream together with fork or fingers, then gradually work in flour. Push dough out with heel of hand. If sticking, add a little more flour. If dry, add a spoon of water. Roll on floured board into circle, or pat directly into 10-inch tart shell or 9-inch pie shell, pressing edge slightly over pan to prevent shrinking. Prick pastry all over with fork. Bake on low shelf of oven until browned, about 12 minutes. Fill as for Fresh Fruit Pie.

Tip: Double recipe, form and freeze the extra shell, unbaked, for future use.

PINEAPPLE RICE PUDDING

Preparation Time: 9 minutes
Cooking Time: None

1 *cup cold cooked rice*
Dash of salt

1 *can (about 5 ounces)*
   crushed pineapple
1 *cup heavy cream*

Have all ingredients thoroughly chilled. Combine rice and pineapple and blend well. Whip cream, fold in. Chill until serving time.

Makes 4 servings.

PINEAPPLE

Preparation Time: 5 minutes
Cooking Time: None

Fresh pineapple is another centerpiece fruit that ripens into dessert. Cut it to serve as its own container for any of these desserts.

PINEAPPLE RAFTS

Cut medium pineapple in quarters, cutting through the green frond so that a section remains attached to each quarter. Cut hard core section from center, using serrated knife. Cut between meat and shell with grapefruit knife, then cut down meat to separate into chunks. Sprinkle with crème de menthe if desired. Serve with picks.

Makes 4 servings.

PINEAPPLE SURPRISE

Halve pineapple lengthwise, cutting through leaves at the top. Scoop out meat, leaving ¼-inch shell. Cube meat, discarding core. Replace pineapple cubes in shell. Add berries or other fruit to fill. Sweeten to taste with sugar, soda or liqueur, or top with ice cream.

Makes 4 to 8 servings.

PEAR HELENE

Preparation Time: 6 minutes
Cooking Time: 3 minutes

For each serving, place a scoop of vanilla ice cream in bottom of sherbet dish. Top with canned pear half. Heat chocolate syrup, pour over and serve immediately. Traditional topping: a candied violet on top of the sauce. No great loss if you skip that.

RHUBARB AND STRAWBERRIES

Preparation Time: 6 minutes
Cooking Time: 8 minutes

1 *pound rhubarb*   ½ *pint strawberries, hulled*
2 *cups sugar*   *and washed*

Wash rhubarb well, cut off leaves and stem ends. Cut rhubarb stalks into 1-inch pieces, discarding any tough strips of outer skin. Do not peel otherwise. Place rhubarb in saucepan and sprinkle with sugar. Cover and bring to boil. Boil about 5 minutes, until rhubarb is tender and syrup has formed. Add strawberries. Bring to boil. Remove from heat. Serve warm or chilled. Great with whipped cream or ice cream.

Makes 6 servings.

STRAWBERRIES OR BLUEBERRIES DEVONSHIRE

Preparation Time: 5 minutes
Cooking Time: None

¼ *pound cream cheese*
½ *cup sweet cream*

1 *pint strawberries or blueberries*

Beat cream cheese with cream to make a thick, creamy topping.
Serve with fresh or frozen strawberries or blueberries.
Makes 4 servings.

STRAWBERRIES IN RED WINE

Preparation Time: 9 minutes
Cooking Time: None

1 *pint strawberries*
¼ *cup vanilla-flavored confectioners' sugar*

1 *cup red wine*

Wash and hull strawberries. Toss with confectioners' sugar.
Spoon into 4 dessert plates. Pour ¼ cup red wine over each
portion. Let stand a few minutes for sugar to dissolve, flavors
to mellow.
Makes 4 servings.

Note: To flavor sugar, keep a vanilla bean in the canister or
jar of confectioners' sugar.

STRAWBERRIES ROMANOFF

Preparation Time: 18 minutes
Cooking Time: None

1 *quart strawberries*
¼ *cup Cointreau or brandy*

1 *pint heavy cream, whipped*
1 *pint ice cream, softened*

Wash and hull strawberries, then dry on paper towels. Separate the less perfect berries and cut them in half. Toss berries with 2 tablespoons liqueur. Whip cream, gently whip into ice cream. Add remaining liqueur. Lightly combine ice cream mixture with cut strawberries. Fold in whole berries, reserving a few of the most perfect for garnish. Spoon into brandy snifters or goblets. Cover, if possible, to allow aroma to develop. Serve immediately or chill.

Makes 8 servings.

STRAWBERRIES TO DIP

Preparation Time: 8 minutes
Cooking Time: None

1 *pint strawberries*　　　　*Confectioners' sugar or yogurt*

Wash berries but do not hull. Arrange around rim of each dessert plate. Place mound of confectioners' sugar or small bowl of yogurt in center. Pick up each berry by stem, dip in and bite off.

Makes 4 servings.

SYLLABUB

Preparation Time: 14 minutes
Cooking Time: None

2 *teaspoons instant coffee*　　1 *cup heavy cream*
½ *cup sugar*　　　　　　　　12 *ladyfingers*
1 *egg white*　　　　　　　　*Fruit*
Pinch salt

Combine instant coffee and sugar. Beat egg white with pinch of salt until stiff but not dry. With same beater, whip 1 cup heavy cream until thick. Gradually whip in coffee-sugar mixture. Fold egg white into whipped-cream mix. Line individual dessert glasses with ladyfingers. Cover with fresh or canned fruit and pile on the syllabub.

Makes 4 servings.

WHIPPED LOW-CALORIE TOPPING

Preparation Time: 12 minutes
Cooking Time: None

⅓ *cup nonfat dry milk*   1 *tablespoon lemon juice*
¼ *cup very cold water*   *Low-calorie sweetener to taste*

Combine all ingredients and beat or blend until thick and fluffy. Makes about 1⅓ cups.

ZABAGLIONE

Preparation Time: 4 minutes
Cooking Time: 6 minutes

2 *egg yolks*   *Sponge fingers or macaroons*
6 *tablespoons sugar*
6 *tablespoons Marsala or*
  sherry

Set double boiler or deep bowl over hot water. Place on gentle heat. Put yolks into the pan or bowl with sugar and Marsala. Using a wire whisk, whisk mixture over low to moderate heat until foamy and thick. Pour into small goblets and serve with sponge fingers or macaroons.

Makes 2 to 4 servings.

Dessert Sauces

CHOCOLATE SAUCE

Preparation Time: 2 minutes
Cooking Time: 7 minutes

⅔ cup hot water
1 package (6 ounces) semi-
    sweet chocolate pieces

½ teaspoon vanilla
Dash salt

Combine all ingredients and heat, stirring until smooth. Serve hot or cool; stir occasionally while cooling.
    Makes about 1½ cups.

Variation: Use ¼ teaspoon mint extract in place of vanilla.

BERRY OR FRUIT SAUCE

Preparation Time: 3 minutes
Cooking Time: None

1 package (10 ounces) frozen
    raspberries, strawberries or

other fruit

Thaw slightly. Spoon into container of electric blender. Add dash of almond extract or lemon extract if desired. Blend smooth.
    Makes about 1 cup.

COFFEE SYRUP

Preparation Time: 4 minutes
Cooking Time: None

1 cup sugar

1 cup strong, hot coffee

Heat and stir until sugar is dissolved and mixture is syrupy.
    Makes 1 cup.

MOCHA SAUCE

Preparation Time: 5 minutes
Cooking Time: 5 minutes

1 *package* (6 *ounces*) *semi-sweet chocolate pieces*

¾ *cup hot coffee*
⅛ *teaspoon salt*
1 *tablespoon butter*

Heat together, stirring often, until smooth. Serve warm. Makes 1¼ cups.

RAISIN-RUM CHOCOLATE SAUCE

Preparation Time: 2 minutes
Cooking Time: 2 minutes

1 *cup raisins*
½ *cup rum*

2 *ounces semisweet chocolate*

Combine raisins, rum and semisweet chocolate in saucepan. Stir over very low heat until chocolate is melted. Serve hot, over ice cream or plain cake.
Makes about 1 cup.

YOGURT PARFAIT

Preparation Time: 3 minutes
Cooking Time: None

In parfait glass, layer alternate spoonfuls of skim-milk yogurt and berries or orange sections or diced cantaloupe in season. Or alternate with raisins or granola. Top with a spoonful of honey. Serve immediately.

For additional desserts, see also Chapter 9 and Chapter 13.

15 Gifts from Your Kitchen for Your Friends or Yourself

CHEESE SPREAD OR TOPPING

Preparation Time: 6 minutes
Cooking Time: None

Use as an appetizer spread or to make grilled sandwiches.

½ *pound Cheddar, grated or blue cheese crumbled*
½ *pound butter, at room temperature*

1 *tablespoon Worcestershire sauce*

Combine cheese, butter and Worcestershire, beating with a fork until smooth and blended. Pile into pint crock or pottery bowl. Keeps in refrigerator for weeks.

CRANBERRY SAUCE PLUS

Preparation Time: 12 minutes
Cooking Time: None

Excellent with poultry, meats, cheeses or as part of sandwich filling.

1 *pound cranberries*
2 *small navel oranges*

1½ *cups sugar*

Wash cranberries, removing any stems. Put through meat grinder or blender to chop. Meanwhile, wash oranges and cut, unpeeled, into quarters. Put through grinder. Add 1½ cups sugar, or to taste, stir well to dissolve sugar, and pile into serving bowl or jar. Keeps well in the refrigerator.

Makes about 4 cups.

Tip: Add another fruit if you like—apple, pear, pineapple, raisins are all good. So is ½ cup of nuts, chopped or put through the grinder with the fruit.

HOT MUSTARD SAUCE

Preparation Time: 5 minutes
Cooking Time: None

4 *tablespoons dry mustard*
2 *tablespoons cold water*
1 *tablespoon sugar*
¼ *teaspoon salt*

1 *tablespoon vinegar*
4 *tablespoons white wine*
1 *tablespoon oil*

Stir mustard with water until free of lumps. Add remaining ingredients and stir smooth. This makes a thin, very hot sauce that will thicken upon standing.

Makes about ½ cup.

PESTO SAUCE

Preparation Time: 5 minutes
Cooking Time: None

Make this in the summer, when basil plants have reached their peak in the garden or in a flower pot on the windowsill. Use to toss with spaghetti and to season cooked fish or poultry or rice.

1 *cup basil leaves*
¼ *cup parsley leaves*
2 *garlic cloves, cut*
¼ *cup pine nuts or walnuts*

¼ *cup grated Parmesan cheese*
½ *cup olive oil*
Salt, pepper

Wash leaves well, discarding any tough stem ends. Place in blender container with garlic cloves, nuts, cheese, oil, salt and pepper. Blend about 15 seconds, until smooth, scraping down sides as necessary.

Makes about 1 cup. Freezes well.

MINT SAUCE

Preparation Time: 5 minutes
Cooking Time: 4 minutes

Another summer special to prepare when mint is plentiful in the garden or growing in a pot on the windowsill. Use with lamb, ham or poultry.

½ cup fresh spearmint leaves   *½ cup water*
½ cup vinegar   *½ cup sugar*

Chop mint leaves or snip with a scissors. Combine in small saucepan with vinegar, water, sugar. Heat, stirring, just to a boil, until sugar is completely dissolved. Store in covered container. Keeps well in the refrigerator.

Makes about 1¼ cups.

LEMON CHEESE

Preparation Time: 7 minutes
Cooking Time: 7 minutes

Use to top a plain cake or ice cream, to pour over berries, to spread on muffins—or eat it with a spoon.

6 tablespoons butter   *¼ cup lemon juice*
¾ cup granulated sugar   *3 eggs*
2 teaspoons grated lemon rind

Place butter in top of double boiler. Add sugar, lemon rind and juice. Beat eggs and strain into pan. Stir constantly over moderate heat until thickened; do not boil. Remove from heat. Pour into serving bowl or jar and cool to thicken further. Keeps well in refrigerator.

Makes 1¼ cups.

16 *Twelve Memorable Dinner Menus*

(SEE INDEX FOR RECIPES)

Spring

Dinner for Two

Artichoke Hearts à la Grecque
Lamb Chops Diane
Risotto
Watercress Salad
Strawberries in Red Wine

Last Minute Supper

Antipasto
Chicken Scaloppine
Spinach Noodles
Raw Mushroom Salad
Granita

Fresh Catch

Mushroom Soup Epicure
Fish Fillets in Wine
Asparagus with French Dressing
Parsleyed Boiled Potatoes
Rhubarb and Strawberries

Summer

Light and Lovely

Salmon Slices
Vegetables Ali Baba
Pappadums
Fresh Peaches and Ice Cream

Cookout

Vegetable Crudités
Shish Kebab
Zucchini with Rice
Cantaloupe
Iced Tea

Cool and Elegant

Guacamole
Shrimp and Snow Peas
Bulgur Pilaf
Sliced Tomatoes with Basil
Mousse Cooler

Autumn

Harvest Supper

Pork and Apple Skillet
Ratatouille
Pears and Cheese
Cider

Brunch Party

Gazpacho (spike with vodka if desired)
Cheese Puff
Bacon Strips
Apple Crisp
Cocoa

Cook It at the Table

Broth Bowls
Sukiyaki
Rice
Pineapple Rafts
Tea

Winter

Warmer-upper

Meatball Soup
Corn Muffins
Bananas Flambées

Buffet Party

Jambalaya with Rice
Bean Salad
Holiday Salad
Fruit and Cheese Tray
Irish Coffee

Six for Supper

Flank Steak
Groats and Corn
Green Bean Salad
Nuts and Wine

17 *Seven Menu Patterns for Low-Calorie Meals*

Choose one basic high-protein dish from eggs, fish, poultry or meat for each meal. Have five fish meals each week. Add to this one low-calorie vegetable or salad, and have all you want of those foods. Choose one Vitamin C fruit and one other fruit for dessert or snack each day, and if you have a taste for lavish desserts, memorize the recipe for Low-Calorie Whipped Topping, page 224. Plan on meals you enjoy, and having enjoyed, leave the table, the kitchen, and eating, until the next meal planned according to your pattern.

Seven Menu Patterns

1 *Early Starter*

BREAKFAST
½ Grapefruit
Broiled Fish Steak
Coffee or Tea

CARRIED LUNCH
Raw Mushroom Salad
Hard-Cooked Egg
Ladyfinger
Glass of Skimmed Milk

SOUP BOWL SUPPER
Chrysanthemum Pot
¼ cup Boiled Rice
4 Chilled Lychees

II *Light Eater*

BREAKFAST
Fresh Strawberries with Skimmed-Milk Ricotta Cheese
   sprinkled with Wheat Germ
Black Coffee

LUNCH
Salade Niçoise (omit anchovies)
Glass of Skimmed Milk

DINNER
Shirred Eggs Florentine (use skimmed milk in place of
   cream)
Yogurt Parfait

III *Snacker*

A.M.
Fresh Apple Sauce (made with sugar substitute)
Slice of Skimmed-Milk Mozzarella Cheese

MID-MORNING
Tomato au Bleu

LUNCH BREAK
Vegetable Crudités
Yogurt

DINNER
Skewered Scallops
Green Salad

EVENING
Melon and Cold Turkey, Prosciutto Style (1 or 2 slices)

iv *Dessert Fiends*

BREAKFAST
2 Crêpes Filled with Ricotta Cheese

LUNCH
Pineapple Half, Filled with Berries and Yogurt

DINNER
Chicken Moo Goo Gai Pan
Applesauce Whip (made with egg whites and artificial
  sweetener)

EVENING
Irish Coffee with Low-Calorie Whipped Topping

v *Hearty Appetite*

BREAKFAST
Whole Orange Cut in Quarters
Hamburger on 1 Slice Bread with Lettuce
All the Tea or Coffee You Want

LUNCH
Whole 3-ounce Tin of Tuna, Bean Sprouts, Lettuce,
  Celery, Cucumber, Green Pepper, Radishes, All
  Sprinkled with Soy Sauce.
1 Waffle with Cottage Cheese
Lemonade Made with Artificial Sweetener

DINNER
Broiled Chicken Oregano
Broccoli
Broiled Tomatoes and Onions

vi *Night Snacker*

BREAKFAST

Skipping this won't help. Try a night-type dish such as
Clam Dip (see Diet Note) with 1 slice of toast cut
into 4 strips, as dippers.

LUNCH

Zuppa Pavese—skip the French toast and nibble on
some raw mushrooms instead

DINNER

Sukiyaki with Water Chestnuts. Linger over this dish.
Have as many water chestnuts as you like.
Chilled Mandarin Orange Sections and Pineapple
Wedges. Set out on platter with ice, nibble from a
pick, 1 at a time. Nibble nothing else!

NIGHT SNACK

Carrot Sticks; Low-Calorie Rice Wafers

vii *Too-Tired-to-Cook*

BREAKFAST

Whole Tomato with Cottage Cheese
Whole-Wheat Crisp Bread

LUNCH

Tin of Sardines, with Lemon Wedge
Canned Asparagus, a little of sardine oil dribbled over
Pear

DINNER

Red Peppers (no anchovies)
½ Barbecued Chicken (purchased)
Classic Green Salad
½ Cantaloupe

Index